THE CULTURAL CONTEXT

OF THINKING

A comparative study of
Punjabi and English boys

Paul A.S. Ghuman

NFER Publishing Company L

Published by the NFER Publishing Company Ltd.
2 Jennings Buildings, Thames Avenue,
Windsor, Berks, SL4 1QS
Registered Office: The Mere, Upton Park, Slough, Berks, SL1 2DQ
First published 1975
© P.A.S. Ghuman
ISBN 0 85633 078 7

Typeset by Jubal Multiwrite Ltd.,
66 Loampit Vale, Lewisham SE13 7SN
Printed in Great Britain by
King, Thorne and Stace Ltd., School Road, Hove, Sussex BN3 5JE
Distributed in the USA by Humanities Press Inc.,
Hilary House—Fernhill House, Atlantic Highlands,
New Jersey 07716 USA.

DEDICATION

This work is dedicated to the memory of my parents.

Contents

LIST OF TABLES

ACKNOWLEDGEMENTS

During the years since I commenced my investigations in this field I have had considerable assistance and encouragement from a number of people.

For their valuable comments and criticism I would like to thank Professor Peel (Birmingham School of Education) and Professor Stones (Liverpool School of Education).

Such a project relies heavily on the goodwill of teachers and pupils; I had excellent cooperation both from teachers and pupils, in Birmingham and Jullundur. I would also like to thank my colleagues at University College of Wales Aberystwyth; Dr Evans for his help in the construction of the attitude scale, Miss Lutkins for her assistance in statistical analysis and Mr Gallop for his interest and encouragement.

My thanks are also due to Mr Carim, Editor of the NFER Publishing Company, for his encouragement and interest in this project. Finally, I am indebted to my wife, Anne, for reading and commenting on the various drafts of this book.

FOREWORD

Dr Ghuman presents an account of research in an important contemporary field — that of the qualities of thinking revealed by different cultural and ethnic groups in our multi-racial society. By a careful choice of groups of children to be tested he was able to examine the effects of the British social and school situation on the development of thinking processes of Punjabi children. He tested Punjabi children living in this country and a group of similar children in the Punjab who had not come into contact directly with life and school in the United Kingdom.

In what follows he gives a readable account of a basic research study. His choice of material is judicious and drawn from a wide range of sources in Cognitive Psychology and enabled him to look for qualitative as well as quantitative differences in thinking.

His most important result is that the thinking processes of Punjabi boys living in England were very similar, both quantitatively and qualitatively to those of native English children, and from this he deduces that the influence of the British environment on the Punjabi children is very powerful even when they have not been in the country very long. There were marked difference between the British and indigenous Punjabi pupils and this he attributed to the poor educational experiences which characterize the rural Punjabi environment. By careful control of the choice of his two Punjabi groups he was able to assure himself that the observed differences in thinking processes were due to cultural and educational environments rather than genetic factors.

Although this book reports a basic research study, it nonetheless relates the findings effectively to the work of well-known theorists in this field

E.A. Peel
Professor, University of Birmingham School of Education

Introduction

Since the influx of peoples from all over the world into Britain during the sixties many schools in our cities have become multi-racial in character. A substantial number of schools now count amongst their pupils children from some of the most ancient cultures and nations on Earth, as well as from some of the newest. Children of all skin colours speaking different languages, practising different religions and nurturing different value systems are being educated alongside native children. Adults and children, who may have never considered other cultures at all, or who may have regarded their own as the only valid one or who may even have definitely regarded other cultures unfavourably, are now face to face with all kinds of differences. But, says Bullock (1975, p. 286), 'Many schools in multi-cultural areas turn a blind eye to the fact that the community they serve has radically altered over the last 10 years and is now one in which new cultures are represented'.

Probably the most important link between different cultures is the teacher to whom these very differences pose a special challenge. Not only must he cope with all the usual aspects of teaching, he also has to cope with the extra problems involved in teaching English as a second language; he will have to introduce immigrant children to the culture of the host community in an acceptable way and provide all kinds of learning experiences lacking in their homes; and he will have to try to form these children of diverse cultures into a workable school group. All this without offending anyone's sensibilities, without creating conflicts and without, however unintentionally, damaging anyone's deeply-held beliefs and customs. Obviously then, it is vitally important that teachers in multi-racial schools should both understand and appreciate the social and religious backgrounds of the minority communities with which they are concerned. For example, the West Indian dialect should not be confused with grammatically poor English; it is a language in its own right and too often children from the West Indies have been hindered in their progress by this misunderstanding. 'A positive attitude to West Indian dialect — as to West Indian culture — would help children and teachers alike in multi-racial city schools. This should receive attention in both initial and in-service teacher training' Bullock (1975, p. 287).

When discussing methods appropriate to the teaching of children from minority groups, the description 'immigrant' is of little use since it is too general, covering a multiplicity of groups. Even the term Asian, used to signify newcomers from India, Pakistan, Ceylon and Kenya is not much more informative because it covers cultural differences as great as those between widely separated European countries. While few teachers now confuse West Indian with Indian (although this does happen), or even Indian and Pakistan (though I have often been asked 'How do you know if they are Indian or Pakistani?'), it is much less understood that there exist considerable cultural differences between a Punjabi and, for example, a Bengali or a Madrasi. Since my research is here concerned with Punjabi Sikhs, my remarks and oberservations refer only to this group and should not automatically be taken to be appropriate to other Indian groups in Britain.

This realization and recognition of the identity of the group is not only important to the child's self-image, it is also vital to the understanding necessary for a fruitful pupil-teacher relationship. For example, the placing of one small Pakistani boy in a class of forty Sikhs, by a well-meaning Head who thought that because he 'looked the same', he belonged to the group, caused the child to suffer a miserable isolation which was only ended when he was removed to an ordinary class comprised of several nationalities where he no longer stood out as the odd one!

While, during the last decade, a number of works dealing with the broad social and cultural background of some immigrant communities have been published, comprehensive works, relating social background to educational possibilities of a specific group, are rare. This monograph explores the social and cultural background, child-rearing practices and acculturation of Punjabi Sikhs in Birmingham and Nottingham, through practical observation in the schools and in their homes where my ready acceptance as a member of the group facilitated questioning and documentation of the upbringing of a Punjabi Sikh in Britain today.

It seems to me that this kind of investigation is particularly important in view of the conclusions drawn by researchers in the field of home/school relationships (Plowden, Douglas), i.e. that the academic achievement of children depends on the stimulation provided by the home and family, the attitude of parents to learning and the value which they place on education, and on their active support to their children coupled with their willingness to participate in school activities. Furthermore, there is now a good deal of evidence relating child-rearing practices to the scope and style of the language acquired by the child and to different methods of problem-solving, thinking and feeling. Indeed, teachers are well aware of the different social and intellectual experiences of native children of different social classes, and it follows then that children coming from diverse cultures and sub-cultures will have even wider differences in their backgrounds which create diffferent learning styles and ways of thinking.

From time to time teachers are required to assess the abilities of pupils and their achievement, for records or diagnostic purposes or for streaming and setting. The standard practice was, indeed it still is, to use established tests of intelligence and abilities. However, research in this area has shown the shortcomings of applying these tests to immigrant children especially when they have had little schooling in this country (Vernon, 1969; Pidgeon, 1970). With non-European children the results of standardized IQ tests are both unreliable and invalid. This is largely due to the children's poor command of the English language, their unfamiliarity with the test material and the test situation, and to poor motivation. The myth of the culture-free test is now clearly exposed (Richardson *et al.*, 1972): since intelligence develops with the support of the culture and is expressed through its artefacts, culture-free would be intelligence-free.

It is worth mentioning here, though, that the IQ scores of various groups of immigrant children increase with the length of their stay in this country (details of this will be discussed in the next chapter). A further, and to my mind serious, shortcoming of this type of test is the excessive emphasis it lays on the product of thinking (correct/incorrect answer), rather than on the ways in which children have reasoned-out their answers, and does not provide the teacher with sufficient constructive information or guide-lines to monitor his teaching. It is for these reasons that the researches of Jensen and others, which are based on standardized tests of intelligence, have little to say about the nature of the thinking processes and are largely irrelevant for the teaching of ethnic minorities.

The limitations of standardized tests have led researchers and educationists who are keen to understand the nature of children's thinking, and especially those in the field of cross-cultural studies, to turn to Piaget's theories of child development. Piaget's theories have been thoroughly researched in this country by, amongst others, Peel (1960), Lovell (1961) and Lunzer (1973), and their implications for education are now well-documented. In addition, his theories have guided researchers in the cross-cultural field in many countries to understand better the thinking processes of children. Since this research is largely based on Piaget's theories and Bruner's elaborations of them it is appropriate to discuss briefly the outline of these models and their relation to this study.

Piaget maintains that children develop their thinking abilities through their interaction with their environments and pass through various stages before reaching maturity in their thinking and judgement. According to him there are four major stages in development: sensori-motor; pre-operational; concrete operations; and formal operations. In the first stage (up to 2 years) the child acquires the ability to co-ordinate sense and movement from which emerge some of the important concepts about his physical environment. The child constructs the concept of the permanence of objects (that things have an identity whether in view or not); the idea that there is objective time, i.e. that events are dependent on things other than himself, and develops some understanding of cause and effect, e.g. that the movement of objects can be effected by things other than himself. Piaget stresses that these ideas of time and objects are not innate, but are constructed by the child as a result of his actions.

In the next, pre-operational, stage (2—7 years) children become capable of representing objects through 'images' and symbols and begin to organize their ideas about the physical world through concepts which, however, are very rudimentary. At this stage, though, children are still very much tied to the contexts of objects and cannot distinguish the real from the apparent change in them, e.g. in conservation experiments children of this age-range think that the quantity, weight and volume of a piece of clay or similar material changes whenever the shape changes. At this stage, too, children find it difficult to deal with problems, e.g. sorting tasks, when more than one attribute is required. During the next, concrete, stage children acquire the ability to conserve quantity, length, weight and later volume, and they learn to deal with problems involving two criteria at once. In short, their thinking is characterized by operations (internalized actions which are reversible) which can, however, be applied only to the concrete reality and not yet to hypothetical situations. In the final stage children can reason with propositions and can apply their thinking to hypothetical situations. They can solve problems by formulating hypotheses and testing them systematically. As this is the highest stage of thinking it is likely that a number of children may never develop as far as this.

All children, according to Piaget, pass through these stages of development invariably in the order described above, but the age at which any stage will be reached depends upon factors within the individual, i.e. biological and psychological, and upon factors in the social and physical environment (Piaget, 1966). This is necessarily a brief outline of Piaget's model and the interested reader can consult texts such as Peel (1960) and Beard (1972).

Another model which has been used in cross-cultural studies is that of Bruner (1967a), which is closely related to Piaget's views. The main principles of his model are twofold. First, Bruner argues that human beings have acquired three distinct but related modes of knowing. The development of these three modes, namely the enactive, the iconic and the symbolic, depends on the socio-cultural stimulation as well as on the extent of which children are encouraged to explore the similarities and the differences between each of the three modes. In the enactive stage the child processes information through his actions. The child's notion of objects is based on what the objects do and/or what the child can do with them. Thus, car is 'brm-brm', hole is 'to dig', cat is 'miaow'. The second style of thinking is marked by the use of imagery. Children begin to form concepts which are relatively free from their actions and situations. However, the surface qualities of objects, which are mostly perceptual in nature, still play an important part in thinking and concept formation. The third mode is characterized by the use of symbols for ordering and structuring experiences, thus liberating the child from 'here and now'. At this stage language as a major activity of man becomes an important instrument of thinking.

The development of these three modes of representation depends upon three elements of culture — type of environment (rural/urban), language system and value systems (religion, myths, conventions). By and large rural environments are simple: their social systems are based on personal interaction, therefore the network of relationships is limited; there is limited access to technology. As a result, there are relatively few demands made upon children to operate at an abstract level. In contrast, children growing up in an urban environment have to make adjustments to a complexity of impersonal relationships and a network of communications. Hence for effective adaptation children learn to think in more abstract terms. Language helps the learner to codify and structure his experiences and thus aids the learner to develop an abstract style of thinking. Furthermore, language can become an instrument for the exploration of physical and social experiences, when the two are deliberately, through instruction, interrelated.

Lastly, the third factor (value-orientation) refers to those key ideas which a society holds regarding the nature of time and space, the nature of Man's existence, and recognized sources of knowledge. Communities which rely on traditional authority for knowledge (elders and religious books, for example), emphasize rigid conformity to group norms resulting in a lack of individuality of thought, action and feeling. Whereas individualized perceptions are, it seems to me, important to the growth of an abstract and analytical style of thinking.

Thus Bruner's model goes a long way towards specifying the nature of social factors important for the development of thinking and I consider it a useful model on which the present research can be based and interpreted.

This research was planned to study the effects of a European type of environment and education on the thinking abilities of Punjabi children. As mentioned earlier, I shall fully describe the child-rearing practices of the Punjabi family from my field work and the religious, cultural and social background of Punjabi Sikh immigrants. As a background, to complete the picture, I shall also set out in some detail the educational system in Punjab, so that the reader may fully appreciate the great contrast between the two educational systems.

The precise aims of this investigation were as follows:

(a) To assess the influences of English schooling (education) on the thinking processes of British Punjabi boys by comparison with control groups in Punjab and England.

(b) To study the thinking processes of Punjabi boys in Punjab and relate such processes to their social milieu.

(c) To assess the degree of acculturation of the families of the British Punjabi sample and relate it to their intellectual abilities.

(d) To compare the scholastic achievement and attitudes to school of British Punjabi boys, as rated by class teachers, with the English control group.

(e) To interpret the results within the developed theoretical framework.

Review of Previous Researches

In this chapter, I shall discuss the previous researches concerning the abilities of immigrant children so that the present research may be meaningfully related to them. As the main concern of this monograph is with the education of migrant Punjabi children, researches relating to their abilities would be analysed in greater detail so that the findings of these can be fully included in our final discussion.

In this country researchers working with immigrant children have largely been concerned with two interrelated questions: (1) Do the abilities of immigrant children differ from those of the indigenous children? If so, in what ways? (2) What, if any, is the effect of British environment and schooling on the basic abilities of these children? There are a number of studies which throw light on both these issues.

The pioneering work was undertaken by Saint (1963) in Smethwick where he studied the intelligence and reading ability of Punjabi speaking secondary school boys. Intelligence was tested by Raven Progressive Matrices and reading ability was assessed by the standard reading tests: a positive correlation (some relationship) was found between the length-of-stay in this country and the test scores. However, the performance of the Punjabi sample was significantly lower than that of the native British children, i.e. the differences between the two groups was real and could not be explained by the element of chance. But it is worth noting that none of the Punjabi boys studied had received primary education in this country and furthermore, the social class backgrounds of the boys were not matched. These two factors are now recognized to be important if valid comparisons are to be made.

Bath (1970) in his investigation of Punjabi secondary school boys found a significant correlation between the length-of-stay and the scores on Raven Matrices, but did not find any relationship between length-of-stay and performance on Schonell Reading and Spelling Test.

It is interesting to note that Bath found that 55 per cent of these children's teachers thought that the boys showed special aptitude for mathematics and 15 per cent remarked on their ability in pottery. Dosanjh (1969) reported similar findings with Punjabi boys in Nottingham.

Little *et al.* (1968) reported the survey conducted on the abilities of immigrant children in London. The results of the 11+ verbal reasoning, English and arithmetic tests were analysed to compare the performance of immigrant and indigenous pupils. The main findings of the study are summarized thus: (1) The immigrant children who had full primary schooling in this country performed as well as (did not differ significantly from) the native British children in tests of arithmetic and verbal reasoning but not in the English test. (2) Children who did not have full education in this country were significantly inferior to the British children on all the tests. (3) The performance of the children from the West Indies was lower, but not significantly so, than that of the children of other immigrant groups (Indian, Pakistanis, and Cypriots).

Thus the findings of this investigation support the results of previous studies that immigrant children benefit from the English education and that their performance improves on the standardized tests of intelligence and on tests of other abilities.

Ashby *et al.* (1970) tested Scottish and Indian children, of varying length-of-stay, in the Glasgow Verbal Reasoning, Moray House, Raven Matrices and Goodenough Draw-a-man tests. To make valid comparisons between the two groups not only did they match the age and sex of the samples, they also considered children's social class, the important dimension which was not considered by the previous investigators. They found no significant differences (whatever differences that were found could be explained by chance element) between the long-stay group (9 years or more) and native Scottish children on all the tests; but the medium-stay group (4 to 8 years) was significantly poorer (difference cannot be explained by chance factor) than the Scottish children on the Glasgow Verbal Reasoning and Raven Matrices tests. However, the short-stay group (3 years or less) scored significantly lower marks on all the tests, as compared with long-stay and Scottish groups. Indian boys were significantly superior to girls, on all the tests, when their results were anlysed as one composite group. Finally, long-stay Indian children were rated significantly higher on their abilities in mathematics than the Scottish children; this seems to concur with Bath's findings.

Thus the findings of this carefully planned study, along with the researches of Bath and Saint, underline the importance of British schooling on the abilities of Indian immigrant children and reinforce the view, held by many psychologists, that the European type of education is more conducive to the development of mental abilities as understood here.

A number of studies have used the Wechsler Intelligence Scale for Children (WISC) to assess the general intelligence of immigrant children. As this test is mainly used by the psychologists in the child guidance clinic, and is not available for wider use in schools, a brief description of it follows. The test is in two parts: Verbal and Performance. The Verbal part consists of General Information; General Comprehension; Arithmetic; Similarities; Vocabulary. The Performance scale is composed of Picture Completion; Picture Arrangement; Block Design; Object Assembly; and Coding or Mazes. The test is given individually, and separate scores can be worked out on all these sub-tests, or on the two main sections, namely verbal IQ and Performance IQ. An overall IQ of the child can be calculated by combining the scores on the Verbal and Performance sections. The test is designed to measure general intelligence, which is defined by its author in the manual as follows: 'In brief, intelligence is part of a large whole, namely, personality itself. The theory underlying the WISC is that intelligence cannot be separated from the rest of the personality, and a deliberate attempt has been made to take into account the other factors which contribute to the total effective intelligence of the individual' (Wechsler 1949, p. 5). The test was originally devised and standardized in America but a British version of it and the British norms are now available.

A recently published research by Haynes (1971) is of great interest because of its scope. A comprehensive battery of tests, which included the WISC test, to assess the conceptual, number, verbal, spatial and learning ability was used with English and Punjabi children living in Southall. They were marked by age (7 to 8 yrs) and sex, but neither on social class nor length of schooling since the principal aim of the research was not to compare performance but to devise tests of learning abilities. Therefore, the comparisons between the two groups are not entirely valid and the results should be interpreted with some caution.

Haynes found significant differences between the two groups on all the tests, with the exception of Coding and Draw-a-man. The Punjabi scores were extremely low (approximately 15 points below the English norm) on the WISC Vocabulary, Holborn Comprehension, WISC Performance IQ, Object Assembly, Picture Completion, Analogies and Concept Formation; but were closer to the English group on the Staffordshire Arithmetic test and verbal learning syllables devised by Haynes. These differences suggest that the Punjabi children were deficient in their linguistic and conceptual abilities and while the reason for the deficiency in language is obvious, the poor performance on conceptual tests is less so. The reasons may be found in the child-rearing practices of the Punjabi family which I shall discuss in Chapter 4. Briefly though, the explanation lies in the fact that Punjabi parents do not consider it necessary to provide children with the basic training in kinaesthetic and perceptual experiences which are the foundation on which conceptual and spatial ability develops.

An interesting aspect of the study is that the length-of-schooling was significantly related to the language tests but not to the tests assessing perceptual and conceptual abilities. This may be due to the fact that the majority of Punjabi children speak virtually no English on entering school; and it is highly likely that teachers devote most of the time to the teaching of English and little time is left to introduce these children to constructional and perceptual material (e.g. blocks, jigsaws, mazes, shapes).

McFie and Thompson (1970) studied the abilities of West Indian children who were referred to the child guidance clinic by using WISC and Schonell Reading tests. Their performance was compared with a matched group of English children. Significant differences were found between the West Indians and the English on the Picture Completion, Picture Arrangement, Block Designs, Object Assembly and Coding sub-tests. However, the achievement of the West Indian children was comparable to the English children on the Verbal section of the WISC test, with the exception of vocabulary. To assess the influence of the English environment and education, the authors compared the performance of those West Indian children who had arrived in this country when they were five years or younger or who were born here, with those children who had arrived in this country after the age of five. The former group achieved significantly higher scores on Comprehension, Vocabulary and Object Assembly. Furthermore, these early arrivals also scored higher, but not significantly, on Picture Arrangement and Coding, but not on Block Design as expected. The following conclusion is drawn by the researchers: 'It is difficult to agree with the view that the highest priority in education of these children is in the field of language teaching: at least as high priority should be given to teaching with mechanical and constructional toys' (p. 350). The findings of this research are thus similar to the conclusion I drew from Haynes' study.

Finally, a study by Sharma (1971) of Indian children is of great interest because of its precision. He compared the performance of long-stay (7 years 1 month) children with that of short stay (1 year 9 months), using an Indian group in India and an English group as controls. The average age of the children was 10 years and they were matched on social class and sex. They were given the battery of WISC performance tests and coloured Raven Matrices test. As the results of the research are rather lengthy only relevant findings are summarized here: (1) Short-stay children were significantly better on all the WISC Performance tests except Coding, as compared with the children in India. (2) Long-stay children performed significantly better on all the tests as compared with short-stay children. (3) The long-stay Indian children were significantly poorer than the English on the Picture Assembly, Block Design, Object Assembly, Coding and WISC IQ, but not on Raven, Digit Span and Picture Completion. However, when boys and girls were compared separately with the English boys and girls, a different pattern emerged. The Indian boys were poorer only on the Object Assembly, whereas girls scored significantly lower on all the WISC Performance sub-tests, except Block Design. (4) The performance of Indian children who were born in this country was not significantly different from those who had full schooling. Therefore it follows that the Indian children improved their performance with stay; however, they were still not as able as the English children on tests involving perceptual and spatial relationships. This is in agreement with Haynes' (1971) findings on Punjabi children.

This brief review of the researches leads us to conclude that the British environment and schooling does improve the tested abilities of the immigrant children and lends further support to the point of view that, given the right type of educational experiences, children from traditional societies are capable of developing the mental abilities which are valued by contemporary Western society. However, we also note that all the measured abilities are not equally affected. The Indian children (mostly Punjabis in this case) show marked progress on the range of verbal and educational abilities but not on the spatial and perceptual abilities and this was also true of the West Indian children. This deficiency in immigrant children may be due to lack of perceptual experiences at home especially in the early years.

There are a number of investigations which relate child-rearing practices to learning and thinking. The Bernstein (1971) school of thought has shown the ways in which value systems of the family influence the early experiences of the young child, which in turn has a strong effect on the child's learning, thinking and verbal expression. Bing (1965) has demonstrated that a strong degree of mother-child interaction promotes verbal ability, and that a child's interaction with the physical environment promotes spatial ability. Witkin and his colleagues (1962) have developed a theory to explain the relationships between the child-rearing practices and the development of abilities. They argue that parents who use strict child-rearing practices (strict discipline, respect for authority, rigid conformity) tend to develop in their children ways of perceiving and thinking which are context-dependent, i.e. these children, generally speaking, do not analyse and impose structures on their experiences but are guided by their total experiences. On the other hand, children who are brought up with sympathy and understanding learn to analyse, abstract and restructure their experiences. The former type of child is described as field-dependent and the latter as field-independent. This dimension of field-dependence/independence, according to Witkin, can be assessed by the use of block design and Draw-a-man tests.

Dawson (1967) used this framework to compare the cognitive styles (ways of perceiving, thinking and solving problems) of two tribal groups, Mende and Temne, who use differing child-rearing techniques. The Temne use harsh child-rearing practices, whereas the Mende tribe treat their children in a less authoritarian manner. The latter encourage children to be independent, they use deprivation as opposed to physical punishment to discipline children, and are far less traditional in their ways. The experiment was done with adults who were matched by age, sex, occupation and education. The results of the project supported the hypothesis that adults from the Temne are more field-dependent.

Berry (1965) tested Witkin's theory with matched groups of Temne and Eskimo adults. The groups were chosen because they contrast on their methods of bringing up children; the Temne group is extremely strict whereas Eskimos encourage autonomy and independence and emphasize the personal qualities of self-reliance, ingenuity and individualism because of the nature of work they are obliged to do. The subjects were assessed on field-dependence by the Koh's Block Design test and an embedded figure test, and their performance was compared with a control group of Scottish adults. The Eskimos were significantly superior to the Temne but there was no difference between them and the Scots. This result then confirms Witkin's model that harsh child-rearing practices tend to produce field-dependent subjects.

A study by Chiu (1972) compared the cognitive styles of Chinese children with those of American, using various tests of field-dependence. His main hypothesis that Chinese children would show greater field-dependence was borne out. The author suggests that this is due to the severe discipline in Chinese families and excessive reliance on mutual dependence. A recent cross-cultural study by Witkin *et al.* (1974) was conducted in three countries: Holland, Italy and Mexico. In each of the three countries two villages were selected as presenting a contrasting picture with regard to degree of emphasis on conformity to family, religion and political authority. Altogether 100 children were tested on the Block Design, embedded figure tests and two other tests of field-dependence. The major hypothesis of the authors that the children from villages which place less emphasis on social conformity are less field-dependent was upheld. Similar findings have been reported by other research workers in the recent issues of the *International Journal of Psychology* (1970—1975).

In view of these findings it would be extremely interesting to apply Witkin's theory to the study of cognitive styles of children from different ethnic groups in Britain, and relate these styles to child-rearing practices of the respective communities.

Researches based on Piaget's Theory

The researches reviewed so far were largely based on the models of intelligence which rely heavily on objective measurement. The major concern of these models is with the products of thought: correct/ incorrect answers, rather than with the mental processes. Piaget's model, on the other hand, concentrates on the thinking processes and allows for variation in the ways problems are presented and answers elicited from children. As mentioned in the first chapter, Piaget's theories have guided researches in the cross-cultural field in many countries to understand better the thinking of children. In the following pages I shall discuss some of the recent and interesting studies which have a bearing on the present investigation.

Peluffo's (1967) researches were designed to study the effects of milieu change on the thinking of children. He included in his investigations samples from three different backgrounds: (1) Traditional (southern Italy); (2) Modern industrial (Genoa); (3) Transitional, i.e. children who had moved from milieu one to two and had been there for three or more years. The children were given Piaget's tests of conservation of volume, physical causality and proportion. On the test of conservation of volume the children from the traditional milieu were the lowest in performance; only 35.1 could conserve, whereas the percentages of successful transitional and modern industrial children were 60 and 70 respectively. It is clear that the performance of the migrant children is closer to the city children and is significantly different from that of the rural children.

In his second experiment Peluffo explored the understanding of the concept of physical causality. The children were asked questions on the movements of clouds, the sun and the moon. The percentages of children who gave mature answers were: Traditional 10; Modern 60; Transitional 50. The third research was planned to test the children's understanding of the concept of proportion. The results confirmed the findings of previous experiments, though the immigrants were not as successful as the city children. The results of these experiments clearly illustrate the importance of environmental factors on the growth of thinking.

Goodnow (1962) used Piaget's model to compare the thinking abilities of Chinese children with that of European children; and to explore the effects of differing social milieux on the mental development of children. The study was based in Hong Kong. The sample included 148 Europeans, 151 Chinese of high social-economic background and full schooling, and 80 Chinese of low social-economic background and low schooling. Five tests of conservation, amount, weight, length, area and volume were given by trained indigenous research workers. In addition, a test designed to assess the ability to plan ahead (combinatorial reasoning) was given to all the children. No differences were found among the various groups on the conservation tests but the European and the high-class Chinese were better on the advance planning test. Goodnow sums up her results as follows: '. . . Similarities across milieux are far more striking than differences' (p. 21). This investigation seems to support Piaget's claim that his model has a universal application and provides evidence for the importance of socio-cultural factors on some thinking processes.

Price-Williams and his colleagues (1967) have carried out a number of researches in Mexico to study the effect of special experiences on reasoning abilities. The first research was done with pottery-making and ordinary children who were matched by age, socioeconomic background and years of schooling. The children were tested on conservation of number, liquid, amount, weight and volume. The pottery making children were significantly superior in their ability to conserve amount but not so in other tests, although the pottery group conserved more frequently than the control group.

This experiment was repeated in another town with a sample of 32 boys. This time they found the pottery group to be superior on all the five conservation tests; suggesting that there is a possibility of transfer of skills from the conservation of amount to the other tasks relating to the conservation of weight, volume, etc., of the things. It is not valid to draw any definite conclusions from this study as the numbers in the sample are rather small. However, the suggestion is that the skills acquired as a result of direct experience with materials do seem to help the children to advance in their thinking. Thus supporting Peel's (1960) views on the role of experience in the development of concepts.

Researches of Beard (1968), Pool (1968), Prince (1968) and Lloyd (1971) show the importance of Western-type environments on the growth of thinking processes. Beard compared the performance of Ghanaian and English children on Piaget's tests of number and quantity. The Ghanaian sample was from 12 schools and the English sample came from 5 schools; both samples representing the range of socioeconomic levels. The results showed a significant difference (in favour of the English children) between the performance of the two groups; but the children from two of the Ghanaian schools, following a more Western style of education, equalled the performance of the English children from a prosperous area of Birmingham. The most interesting finding, however, was that the younger children from a poor area in this country did less well than the children from the poor areas of Accra. This suggests that researchers in comparative studies should pay special attention to the social backgrounds of the children and not be misled by the overall difference in performance.

Pool assessed the importance of urban versus rural environments on the attainment of scientific concepts among Haussa children of Nigeria. He took samples of children, aged 10 to 11, from three environments: rural, intermediate and urban. A test of 32 items, relating to conservation of time, space and measurement, was given to a total sample of 150 children. The result confirmed the author's hypothesis that the performance of urban children is superior to that of the other two groups. In addition, it was found that the intermediate group was better than the rural group on some of the test items. Lloyd investigated the concepts of conservation of number and quantity with Yoruba children of varying social class backgrounds. An American group of children (whose social background is not given) acted as a control group. The children were tested by native students using familiar and unfamiliar materials. The Yoruba children from higher social class backgrounds performed as well as the American children. However, contrary to expectations, the use of familiar material did not produce better answers from the Yoruba children. Lloyd concludes the report by confirming the validity of Piaget's model and the universal importance of socio-cultural and educational factors in the growth of thinking abilities. A recent investigation by Philp and Kelly (1974) reinforces the view that Piaget's theories are extremely useful in making cross-cultural comparisons. They studied children from three different cultures: (1) Children of Australian born parents living in New South Wales; (2) Children of non-English speaking migrants living in New South Wales; (3) Children from three different areas in Papua and New Guinea. The total sample amounted to 1,536 children, who were given, among other tests, tasks of conservation of quantity and length. The results of the research are rather complex and lengthy but the main finding of interest is summarized by the authors: 'The behaviours described and classified by both Piaget and Bruner were demonstrated to exist among Papua-New Guinea children, whether or not they have gone to school and among, also, New South Wales children, migrant and non-migrant. The exception to this statement is that behaviours described by Piaget as formal operations, did not appear among any of the Papua-New Guinea children in our sample' (p. 263).

A further investigation by Prince (1968) explores the relationship between the degree of exposure to European culture and performance on scientific concepts based on Piaget's theory. Prince administered a group test of 23 items, based on conservation problems and under-standing of scientific concepts, to 2,700 primary and high school children in New Guinea. The results confirmed the expected pattern of Piaget's stages, though conservation was not generally achieved until much later than in Western culture. Further analysis of the results of three samples taken from three districts with varying degrees of Western influence, confirmed the hypothesis of the importance of a Western type of education on conservation tasks. Prince concludes with this remark: '. . . The writer has found no evidence . . . that inheritance particularly affects performance in the tests administered; on the other hand there is clear evidence, with the strongest supporting impression from interviews and all kinds of experiences, that environment is a powerful factor in determining the progress of conceptual development' (p. 73). This conclusion seems to concur with Vernon's plea that:

> '. . . This does not mean that differences between more "primi-
> tive" and more civilized mentalities are due to genetic limitations,
> rather we should look for their origins in the upbringing of the
> children and the nature of society' (p. 19).

However, a more recent investigation by de Lemos (1969) has thrown up some evidence to support the view that genetic factors may be more important than environmental ones. She tested aboriginal children in Australia on tasks of conservation of number, amount, length, weight and volume; and sub-divided her sample into full aboriginals and part-aboriginals — the latter having a small degree of European ancestry. The ages of the children ranged from eight to 15 and the two groups lived in a similar environment. She found that part-aboriginal children were significantly better on four tests of conservation and were superior, but not significantly so, on the other two tests. She concludes: '. . . It would be, therefore, reasonable to attribute the significant differencee between the part and full aborigines in this study to genetic differences between aborigines and Europeans, resulting in the part-aboriginal children having a higher probability of inheriting a higher intellectual potential,' (p. 268). Eysenck (1971) considers this to be an important piece of research which substantiates the case of geneticists. He writes: '. . . on the whole this study must stand as one of many props for the genetic hypothesis which environmentalists will find it difficult to dislodge,' (p. 101).

Contrary to what Eysenck thought, environmentalists have found evidence to put the results of de Lemos' investigation in serious doubt. Dasen (1972) replicated de Lemos' study using a comparable sample in the same cultural setting and utilizing in the main the same tests of conservation. He confirmed de Lemos' findings on the universality of the nature of thinking processes as theorized by Piaget, but his results did not support her findings relating to the significant differences between the performances of full aboriginal and part-aboriginal children on any of the tests. This was despite the fact that he made every attempt to match the instructions, procedures and analyses with the study of de Lemos. Dasen remarks: '. . . None of the values achieve statistical significance. No genetic differences are evident in the acquisition of concrete operations, even when the chances of finding such differences are maximized,' (p. 83). He concludes: '. . . Our results cannot, of course, be taken as conclusive until their contradiction with those obtained by de Lemos has been resolved. However, until this can be done, de Lemos' results should no longer be used to support the argument for genetic differences in mental functioning,' (p. 84). The main conclusions which can be drawn from this brief review of studies are: (1) That the thinking processes which are described by Piaget are to be found universally. (2) Piaget's tests are more suitable as compared with the standardized tests of intelligence. (3) Performance on tests is affected by socio-cultural and educational factors, especially those related to Western European Culture.

Researches based on Bruner's model

Though Bruner's views on intellectual development are closely related to that of Piaget's, there are essential differences. Whereas Piaget seeks his explanations in logical and biological factors, Bruner emphasizes the importance of language and social and cultural factors. Here we review a number of researches which he and his colleagues have undertaken to provide support for the model. Greenfield and Bruner (1966) explored the relationship between language and thinking processes in Senegal. In addition, the possible influence of the value system was also undertaken. The sample collected for the research represented three different degrees of urbanization and schooling. All the children were tested individually on the conservation of amount test and a picture sorting test. In the picture test children were asked to group pictures together which go with each other in some way. The results of the research are most interesting. The researchers found considerable difficulty in making their questions, relating to the conservation test, meaningful to the non-school-going children. Thus the question: 'Why do you think this glass has more water than this one?' had to be asked in the following manner: 'Why is such and such true?' (p. 92). The reason given for this failure to understand the basic question is that in the traditional community individuality is curbed and loyalty to the group is encouraged. Consequently an individual's feelings and thinking are submerged in the group and questions relating to personal judgement are meaningless. Alternatively, it may be argued that in such communities, the stock of knowledge and skills are passed on 'ready-made' to the children in the form of myth and folklore by the elders, who discourage the children from asking questions which challenge the fundamental bases of the tribe's knowledge and practices.

Furthermore, it is interesting to note that some children invoked 'magic' to explain the different levels of water in the containers. However, equally interesting is the fact that school-going children of the Wolof tribe do not display this type of thinking.

On the picture sorting test there was a significant difference between the younger non-school-going and the school-going children. The former tended to suggest their reasons for grouping by pointing to each and every picture whereas the latter used verbal labels for explanations. However, the older illiterate children did use labels more frequently, but their use of the full sentences to describe their reasons for grouping remained very poor; whereas the school-going older children were remarkably better in their ability to do so. The authors inferred from the data that the use of sentences enhanced the children's ability to structure their groupings on imaginative lines and also produced more complex groupings.

Maccoby and Modiano (1969) report the findings of an investigation planned to test the hypothesis that rural children prefer to look for similarities in things on the bases of colour, shape and size (concrete attributes). The study was carried out in Mexico with 12 to 13-years-old children, from rural and urban backgrounds. The children were presented with pictures of common objects and then questioned on their ability to form links between the objects. For example, the children were presented with a picture of a banana, an orange and a bean and were asked the following questions: (1) In what way is a banana the same as an orange? (2) How is a bean different from a banana and an orange? The answers of the children were placed in one of the three categories: (1) concrete; (2) concrete-abstract; (3) abstract. Sixty-nine per cent of the rural children were in the concrete category as compared with 39 per cent of the urban children. The rural children were better at describing the differences between the objects but were really poor in their ability to describe similarities.

In another investigation Maccoby and Modiano (1967) compared the thinking styles of rural Mexican and North American children. The ages of the children ranged from 5 to 17 years. The task was similar to the one described above, but the scoring procedure was on five rather than three categories: (1) Perceptible (colour, shape, size); (2) Functional (what can be done with the objects); (3) Affective (likes and dislikes of objects); (4) Nominal (name of the objects); (5) Decree (because-I-say-so type answers). The younger children (six-to-eight years) from both the cultures were found to be most comparable in their styles; both groups being equally successful in finding differences between the objects. These younger children described the differences by using colour, shape and size (perceptible attributes) of the objects. However, the older American children were better at finding similarities between the objects and in using nominal and functional attributes as compared with the older Mexican children. The authors conclude: '. . . the North American child starts out by seeing objects in terms of perceptible and concrete characteristics, but he soon begins to consider them in the light of what he can do with them . . . In contrast, the Mexican child of six or eight is far more similar to older brothers in terms of intellectual approach' (p. 260). In their second investigation the authors compared the styles of these two groups with those of another group of urban Mexican children. The inference drawn from the data is that twice as many urban as rural Mexican children were successful in finding similarities in the objects at the age of nine, and this difference increased four-fold by the age of 12. They conclude that the performance of the city Mexican children is more like the performance of Boston children in America. Also, they argue that the urban children were abstract in their sorting behaviour unlike the rural children who preferred to group on the basis of concrete attributes.

Evans and Segall (1969) carried out a research on rural Ganda children, who were given two sorting tests: A test with actual objects and a test with the pictures of objects. In both these tests children showed a marked preference to sort the objects on the basis of colour. In another experiment the same two researchers studied differences between rural and urban children on their ability to learn to group objects on the basis of common attributes. A sample of 270 children representing three grades and three degrees of urbanization were tested on 20 sets of four objects. Out of each set two objects were of the same colour, and were functionally related (had common functions) to the third object. The fourth object shared neither the function nor the colour of the other three. The children were split into two groups; half the children having to discover likeness based on colour and the other half on function, and then the order was reversed. The children were reinforced according to the desired criterion. The analysis of the results showed that colour was more rapidly learned than function; that unschooled children compared favourably, on the colour attribute, with schooled children but not on the functional attribute. Lastly, the urban school children performed better than the rural children on the tasks. The authors conclude by saying that the sorting by function task was harder for rural than for urban children, with the children in the most rural school having the greatest difficulty with it. This experiment was repeated with 30 urban and 31 rural adults. The results showed that rural adults were better in learning to classify by colour; whereas urban adults had greater facility in learning to classify by functional attributes. Lastly Serpelo's (1969) investigation with Zambian children of differing rural and urban backgrounds supported the hypothesis that rural children prefer colour for matching objects as compared with urban children.

What has emerged from these researches is that children in rural settings prefer to use concrete rather than abstract categories in their groupings and are less flexible in their approach to the problems. And that models of intellectual development which do not include the socio-cultural dimensions are not likely to offer fuller understanding of the thinking processes of children. In summary, we have found a fair degree of support for Bruner's model in which socio-cultural and linguistic factors are considered important for explaining the development of mind.

Vernon's researches

Piaget, Bruner and Witkin approach their researches from theoretical viewpoints, whereas Vernon's approach is applied. In his researches (1965, 1969), Vernon was not interested in validating a model nor in investigating racial or ethnic differences but in styding the effects of controllable environmental factors on the development of various types of abilities. In his studies he used a wide variety of tests, including verbal and educational, induction, concept development, creativity and perceptual and spatial. The influence of the following factors on the achievement was investigated: regularity of schooling; unbroken homes; economic status of father; cultural stimulus provided in home; male dominance; family planfulness; encouragement of initiative and linguistic background.

The samples included boys from Jamaica, Uganda, Canada (Indian and Eskimo) and the Hebrides Islands off the west coast of Scotland. The ages of the boys ranged from 10½ to 11 years. All the boys were rated on home background variables on the basis of personal interviews. The tests were administered with the help of indigenous research workers individually and on group bases. For example Piaget's battery of tests were given individually, whereas achievement tests were administered to groups.

The Jamaican children were significantly poorer in their performance on Raven Matrices, Koh's Blocks, Form board and Perceptual tests as compared with the representative sample of English boys, but the differences were less marked on Piaget's battery of tests and the Card-sorting test. There were marked sub-cultural differences within the Jamaican sample: the urban children were significantly superior on conceptual tests of ability but not so on achievement tests of arithmetic and English. The author suggests that these differences are due to the home background factors as opposed to type of schooling. Vernon concludes his results: 'Next it is clear that the most important single factor in childrens' performance on "g" and verbal tests is the cultural level of the home, parental education and encouragement, reading facilities and probably the speech background . . . and among West Indians cultural stimulus strongly affects perceptual-practical abilities as well' (1965, p. 128).

The research in Uganda was carried out with boys who lived in Kampala. The age and social backgrounds of these children was slightly higher than those of the Jamaican children. The analyses of the results showed these boys to be specially retarded on Piaget's tests of conservation in three-dimensional interpretation of figures; but not on the spatial-perceptual tests. The background factors which were found to be significant are: socioeconomic status, cultural stimulus in the home, planfulness, unbroken home and initiative.

The Eskimo boys in Canada did specially well on spatial and perceptual tests but not so well in inductive reasoning and Piaget's tests of conservation. The home-background factors of this sample did not correlate with the tests of general ability and scholastic achievement.

All the overseas groups tested on these batteries of tests were significantly poorer than the English group. The author suggests that the handicaps of these groups can be categorized as follows: (a) constitutional; (b) positive environmental factors; (c) extrinsic handicaps due to language and motivation.

The author, rightly, treats the results of these tests cautiously due to the problems of reliability and validity of the instruments. However, he suggests 'more intensive studies of particular aspects of mental development with locally constructed tests within non-Western cultures' (1969, p. 229). Vernon's work has pinpointed some of the factors which influence the development of abilities which have been shown to be of educational significance. He implies that attitudes, value systems, child-rearing practices and democratic family climate, as well as the broad and deep cultural interest of a Western-European middle class culture-type are to be regarded as being most conducive to intellectual development. Vernon recommends the adoption of such norms and values to the people of Africa and West Indies. From a practical viewpoint this is a sound principle, but it raises substantive issues of preserving the languages, cultures and ideologies of other societies.

Vernon's investigations have shown that the development of intellectual abilities depends largely on ecological and socio-cultural factors, i.e. children develop those skills and cognitive processes which are valued by the societies in which they grow up. There is further evidence to support this view from the researches of Lesser *et al.* (1965), which were carried out in America with Negro, Chinese, Puerto Rican and Jewish children. They were administered batteries of tests to assess their verbal and reasoning abilities, number facility and 'Space Conceptualization' ability. The research workers who gave these tests belonged to the same ethnic groups as the children they were testing.

The major purpose of the study was to examine the patterns among various mental abilities in six- and seven-year-old children from different social class and cultural backgrounds. The findings of the studies confirmed the hypothesis that differences in ethnic group membership do produce significant differences in both the absolute level of each mental ability and the patterns among these. From the analyses of the data the authors concluded that social class and ethnic group membership, and their interaction, have strong effects upon the level of each of the four mental abilities. Lastly, it was found that ethnicity has the prime effect on the pattern of mental abilities, and this organization is not altered by social class variations.

The authors explain this differential pattern of abilities by postulating a number of environmental variables, which are similar to the ones discussed by Vernon. They conclude: '. . . In summary, the evidence of strong social class and ethnic group influences upon the level of each mental ability, and the emergence of a pattern of mental abilities specific to each ethnic group that remains unaltered by social class position, lends support to Abastasi's premises . . . "Groups differ in their relative standing on different functions. Each . . . fosters the development of a different pattern of abilities" ' (p. 78).

It is appropriate at this point to discuss the views of Jensen and other psychologists who believe that the differences in intellectual abilities of different ethnic groups are largely due to genetic as opposed to environmental factors. It is argued from the studies of twins and related researches (Jensen 1972, p. 124) that 75 per cent of the variance (total difference in scores of the groups) on the IQ tests can be explained by genetic factors and 25 per cent by environmental factors. This basic finding is applied to explain the difference between the performance of American white and negro children – the negro children, on average, score 15 points below the white.

This technique of proportioning variance to hereditary and environmental factors may be a sound statistical principle, but it is no substitute for psychological or genetic explanation of the processes involved. Piaget (1956) puts it succinctly: '. . . The Psychologist for his part welcomes the qualitative character of logic, since it facilitates the analysis of the actual structures underlying intellectual operations, as contrasted with the quantitative treatment of their behavioural outcome. Most "tests" of Intelligence measure the latter, but our real problem is to discover the actual operational mechanisms which govern such behaviour and not simply measure it' (p. 41). And according to Stott (1960): '. . . The contemporary view of genetic determinants is that there are built-in instructions for the development of the organism within the range of environment for which it is fitted. To ask whether given individual variations are more due to the variability of the instructions or to that of the environment is not to ask one question, but a thousand or a hundred thousand . . . to try to assess either of the two types of influences as percentages, even in individual cases, would be merely rhetorical quantification' (p. 247).

Whatever the pros and cons of the problem, it is desirable to discuss at least one study in detail. In a well-known article Jensen (1971) reports a study in which he controlled the so-called input variables (social class, home background factors, schooling, etc.) to investigate achievement levels and the conceptual and associative types of abilities of Negro, 'Anglo' and Mexican-American children. The scores from the comprehensive battery of tests, designed to assess the above mentioned abilities, were factor analysed. Four factors were extracted: (1) Verbal IQ and achievement; (2) Non-verbal intelligence; (3) Memory; (4) Socioeconomic status. The scores of all the children were worked out on these four factors to detect the differences among groups. The Negro children were found to be significantly inferior to the white children on factors of IQ and non-verbal intelligence, but there was no difference between the two groups on factors of memory and socioeconomic status. Though the Mexican children, according to Jensen, were on the whole inferior to the Negro children on factor 4 (Socioeconomic), on average they were significantly superior in their performance. It is implied, though not mentioned in this article, that this inferior position is due to genetic factors. At any rate Jensen writes: '. . . It seems not unreasonable, in view of the fact that intelligence variation has a large genetic component, to hypothesize that genetic factors may play a part in this picture' (Jensen, 1972, p. 162). If this stance is accepted, it follows from his findings that the Negro children do not possess conceptual ability (Level 2) to the same degree as the other two groups.

The basic assumption of the research is that the Negro children have similar social backgrounds to the children from the other two groups. This may be the case as judged by the social inventory, but not so if we examine the historical backgrounds of the groups. American Negroes were subjected to slavery: their languages, traditions, beliefs and value systems were destroyed; family life was eliminated. It is naive to assume that all these disadvantages can be wiped out in a few generations. Butcher (1972) wrote in reply to Jensen's paper:

'. . . But the difference has been one of caste rather than class and the history of the Negroes in USA, especially in the Southern States, has been one of fear and oppression. Other minority groups such as Mexicans have not suffered slavery and lynching. It would not be astonishing if the memory of such experiences should exercise a general depressive effect on the psychological development of an entire ethnic group . . . there is no reason why within a generation the mean Negro-White difference in measured ability in the USA should not shrink to a comparable degree' (p. 94).

Lastly, the social inventory used to assess the home background factors (Gough, 1949) of the children was constructed in 1949, when our knowledge of the social factors affecting the intellectual and educational development was rudimentary. For instance, the inventory includes such items: Do you have a fireplace in your home? Do you have a bathtub in your home? But there is a lack of items inquiring into (a) conceptual stimulation at home, (b) demanding home background, (c) adjustment of children, (d) perceptual and kinesthetic experiences, (e) linguistic experiences.

It is true to say that material possessions can be relatively easily acquired; but to acquire new value-orientations, aspirations and related attitudes deemed to be necessary for educational achievement, takes a long time, possibly several generations, even in a favoured milieu. An analogous situation existed in India because of the caste system. Though the low castes have been granted equal status in law, and have been given generous economic and educational provision, there is as yet no substantial evidence to suggest that these people have overcome their problems. Considered in this context, the poor performance of Jensen's Negro sample is no surprise to those who subscribe to the importance of environmental factors.

We have covered much ground in the review and it is now appropriate to relate the main points to the present investigation. Piaget's basic theory and technique of investigations, Bruner's emphasis on the importance of linguistic and socio-cultural factors, Witkin's contribution in relating child-rearing practices to perception and thinking and Vernon's specification of the effect of family background on scholastic achievement, have provided useful perspectives on which this project is based.

It became clear during the course of our discussion that, to make valid comparisons between the Punjabi and the English children, we must control variables of sex, social class and length-of-schooling. In addition, a matched group in Punjab is necessary if the effects of the British environment and schooling are to be fully explored. This project takes into account all these factors.

It also emerged from the analysis that the study of the thinking processes of the immigrant children is best undertaken by the use of individual as opposed to group tests of abilities. Furthermore, tests should be given in an informal manner and that the children should be familiar with the test material to secure good motivation. These ideas were incorporated in this research; all the tests, except two, were given individually and due care was also taken to make the test materials meaningful.

Finally, the important role which the family plays in the development of abilities and scholastic progress became clear in our discussion. In this study the home backgrounds of the Punjabi pupils were assessed by a semi-structured interview and it was hoped that such information would be of great value in understanding the abilities of these children.

In the next chapter I shall discuss fully the plan of the experiment which includes the following (1) number and ages of children; (2) control of variables; (3) nature of tests and what they measure; (4) procedure of administration; (5) backgrounds of the samples.

Planning of the Research, Description of the Samples and Tests

In order to test the research questions raised in the first chapter and to explore the socio-cultural background of the Punjabi children, a comprehensive research plan had to be devised. Matched samples of boys from three communities, indigenous Punjabi, immigrant Punjabi, and English, were taken to ascertain the effects of English environments on the thinking abilities of the Punjabi boys in this country; and to assess the home background of these boys an interview schedule was planned.

Girls had to be excluded from the sample because of the problems indigenous Punjabi girls pose to a male research worker. These girls are brought up in strictly traditional ways and are extremely shy and withdrawn and it would have been impossible for a male researcher to obtain meaningful responses from them. Moreover, the increase in sample size necessary to include both boys and girls would have made the study, particularly the field work in Punjab, impracticable. The other factors on which boys were matched included: (1) age, (2) social class, (3) ethnic background (only for Punjabi samples), (4) years of schooling (only applicable to groups in this country).

Two age groups were selected. The first consisted of boys between the ages of nine years nine months and 10 years 11 months and the second was composed of boys between the ages of 11 and 12 years. (For details see Table A1 in Appendix A). It was hoped that this choice would help us to discern developmental trends in the thinking and problem solving of the two Punjabi groups. Regarding social class, a majority of the English (78 per cent) and the immigrant Punjabi boys (90 per cent) — referred to as British Punjabi boys hereafter — came from unskilled and semi-skilled manual backgrounds. (Please see Table A2 in Appendix A for details). However, it was not easy to match the indigenous Punjabi boys on this factor, as the structure of Punjabi society is different from that of the English. This problem was overcome by selecting only those British Punjabi boys whose fathers, prior to emigration, were farmers, although now working in different types of jobs. Similarly, the family background of the boys selected in Punjab was farming. The ethnic background of the boys will be fully discussed in the next chapter. But briefly, the boys belonged to the Jat-Sikh community (incidentally, a very high proportion of immigrant Punjabis from India belong to this group) which has a distinct religious, cultural, linguistic and ethnic identity. This group belongs to the Vaish Caste according to Manu's classification, and has preserved its ethnic identity through marriage within the community. Finally, the factor of schooling was controlled: both the English and the British Punjabi boys had full schooling, i.e. from the age of five onwards, whereas the boys in Punjab start school at the age of seven and could not be matched on this variable.

Social background of the samples

As a consequence of living and working in the city of Birmingham, I was closely involved with the Punjabi community. There are a number of main areas within which the Punjabis from India have settled, evolved their institutions and continued their distinctive style. Handsworth is such an enclave. The population of this borough is largely composed of Punjabi Sikhs, West Indians, Irish immigrants and a few indigenous whites. These ethnic groups live in relative harmony but with very little social mixing, each group having its own favourite places for shopping, eating and entertainment.

A walk down the Soho Road, a main street running through Handsworth, is an interesting experience. Eye-catching shop-windows flank the road whose pavements are crowded with colourful, exotically-dressed women from India and the Caribbean in saris, elegant *salwar-chemise* (Punjabi trouser suits) and sarongs. Almost the only English shops left are those whose goods are universally useful, e.g. furniture, men's clothes, electrical goods, and one or two of the large chain stores (Boots, Woolworth, Burton). Nearly all the others are now owned by immigrants, particularly by Punjabis. There are Indian supermarkets, greengrocers, restaurants, drapers and cinemas showing Indian films. The West Indians too have their own clothing stores, food shops and hairdressers. There are Cypriot fish and chip shops too, but the most comprehensively represented group are the Punjabis. Every kind of North Indian fruit and vegetable is on display, and all the usual 'dry' groceries, − many kinds of pulses, chapatti flours of all sorts, for example − are widely available, so much so that the Indian families do not need to eat any European food unless they wish to do so. The latest styles of women's clothing cram the many drapers' windows which are rainbow-hued with saris of every conceivable colour, chemise fabrics richly decorated, jackets beautifully embroidered and all the accessories which the fashionable Punjabi woman could ever need! And there is an extensive range of children's clothes in Indian style. Nowadays on Soho Road Punjabi families can obtain practically everything that they would have used back home — from their special kind of bedding to wall hangings, from cooking utensils to herbal remedies — exactly as they would have liked to buy in India. Nearby are factories making all kinds of underwear, sari-blouses and other Punjabi clothes. There is an Indian mortgage broker and, in modern style, 'take-away' food shops, selling the full range of Indian sweet and savoury dishes. The Punjabi housewife has very rarely any need to shop anywhere where she needs to speak English. The Post Office usually has one or two Punjabi-speaking counter assistants and other official institutions help in this way too and an Indian doctor can easily be found. There is no social contact with the English; she can carry on her daily life very much as though she were in Punjab. Perhaps this is the reason why the Punjabi women rarely learn much English — even when her husband and children do so — she just doesn't need it.

What has made the Handsworth Punjabis into one well-knit community, in addition to all this, is the establishment of the local temples — the Gurdawara, which is the centre of Sikh cultural, social and religious life. Large numbers of them visit the temples regularly on Sundays to socialize and to worship; women are equally welcomed. Schools are held there on Saturdays for the children to learn their own language and about their culture. Almost all the Sikh marriages and other important ceremonies take place there. Through this institution they have carried on with their native religious beliefs, social customs and habits and indeed have kept in touch with the 'politics' of Punjab. From time to time politicians of various schools of opinion have come over from Punjab to raise funds and to canvass for moral support. I think it would be correct to say that Punjabis have shown a very keen interest in the politics of Gurdawaras and that of Punjab and are less interested in the local and national politics of this country. Thus all in all the temple has played and probably will play a very important part in preserving their way of life and Punjabi identity.

Handsworth is largely designated as an Educational Priority Area because of poor school buildings, linguistic problems and a host of other factors. Thus, it can be argued that boys in this area were receiving a similar type of education and between school variations have been considered to be of little importance. It is also worth mentioning that all the schools included in the sample had more than 60 per cent immigrant pupils. The headmasters of six primary schools in this area were approached, five of whom kindly agreed to provide facilities for research. Boys in Punjab were selected from two village schools which are about 2 to 4 miles distant from the main town of Nawan Shahr (see next chapter).

Size of the samples

By and large it is considered desirable to take fairly large samples for researches; though, according to Burroughs (1971) the exact size should be decided upon by statistical and practical considerations. The numbers in the samples in this study, however, were primarily based on practical rather than statistical grounds.

The size of the samples, to a degree, depends on the type of test to be used for assessment of abilities. For instance, it is possible to test a fairly large number of pupils on group tests, whereas in cases of individually administered tests, samples necessarily have to be smaller. Since the primary purpose of this study was to investigate the thinking processes and their socio-cultural correlates, all the tests, except one, were individually given. Furthermore, it was considered that boys in Punjab would respond better in a face-to-face situation, as they had virtually no experience of doing group tests or formal examinations at the time of testing. Vernon (1969) has followed such a strategy in his cross-cultural researches. Thus the major restriction on the size of the groups was the time available for testing both in Punjab and England. Bearing in mind these limitations it was decided to have the following numbers of the groups:

	Junior age group (9—9+)	*Senior age group (11+)*
English	25	25
British Punjabi (Immigrant)	25	25
Punjabi (Indigenous)	20	20
	70	70

Total 140

Choice of tests, administration of tests and scoring procedures

As the main purpose of this research was to look closely at the thinking processes of boys rather than the product of these processes, it was considered prudent to use as many individual tests as practicable. Two types of tests were included: the first category consisted of tests which can easily be adapted to different cultural settings, e.g. conservation problems and the second category included tests of a more formal nature, e.g. WISC Block Designs, the content, format and administrative procedures of which cannot be altered. This choice was based on the hypothesis that the indigenous Punjabi boys would do relatively well, as compared with the boys in this country, on the tests which are presented to them in materials with which they have previous experiences; but not so well on the tests which are basically developed and standardized in the European context.

Conservation problems

According to Elkind (1968) our notion of Concept is based on one of two basic assumptions: either we acknowledge the differences between the objects, e.g. between a cat and a dog, or we accept a variability within the things and ignore the variability across things, e.g. ice and water have the same composition but vary in state. The behaviourist psychologists largely prefer to use the first model in explaining the processes of concept formation − as for example the definition of Concept in this type of psychology is 'Similar response to dissimilar stimuli', whereas Piaget's notion is based on the second premise. Conservation problems were devised to test the child's understanding of the real and the apparent: what things look like after a change in shape, colour, etc., and what they really are. Thus in the classic sausage experiment (two balls containing the same amount of plasticine are shown to the child, when he is convinced that both have the same amount; one of them is then rolled into a sausage shape and the child is asked whether they have the same amount), the child who responds correctly by saying that the ball and the sausage have the same amount of plasticine has distinguished between the real and the apparent variation. Piaget (1952) considers such an understanding necessary for intellectual development: 'obviously, conservation, which is a necessary condition of all experience and reasoning, by no means exhausts the representation of reality . . . our contention is merely that conservation is a necessary condition for all rational activity' (p. 3). Vernon (1969) considers these tests to be a good measure of concrete stage of thinking: '. . . conservation should give some indication of mental maturity − the attainment of Piaget's stage of concrete operations, though in practice it differs little from induction ability' (p. 140).

Because of the importance of the psychological processes underlying conservation problems and the fact that these have been successfully used in cross-cultural researches, the problems of Conservation of Weight, Area and Volume were included in the test battery. Regrettably, the test of Conservation of Volume had to be omitted with the Punjabi groups because of the limited time available for testing in Punjab.

Conservation of weight

Boys in this country were tested with two balls of clay and a two-pan balance. The balls were placed on the balance pans and the boys were asked to make sure that the two weighed the same. Then one of the balls was flattened into a pancake shape in front of the boys and the following question was asked: 'If I place the flat piece on the scales, is it going to weigh the same, more or less than the ball?' After the boys had given their answers they were asked to give their reason for their answers. Sometimes supplementary questions had to be asked to go beyond what they have said in order to assess their true abilities. The answers were recorded verbatim. The test material for the Punjabi boys in Punjab had to be replaced by mud balls as they had no experience of clay. (Punjabi children generally play with mud, modelling farm animals and household things.) Similarly an Indian type of balance was used; equivalent instructions were given in the Punjabi language and the responses were recorded in Punjabi.

Conservation of area

Two green fields were represented by a large sheet of green blotting paper folded into two halves. The crease showed a clear demarcation between the two fields. The paper was placed on a table with a model cow in one field and a model horse in the other. The boys were told that the two animals have exactly the same amount of grass to eat and they could check if they so wished by folding the paper. Afterwards, they were shown eight model houses of exactly the same design and size, and four were placed on each field; on the cow's field they were placed in a terraced position towards one side; on the horse's field the houses were widely spaced over the field. The boys were asked the following questions: 'Now have the horse and the cow the same amount of grass to eat as each other or different? Why do you think so?'

Boys in Punjab were given the test in exactly the same way but a buffalo and an ox were substituted for the cow and horse, as Punjabi farms rarely keep horses on the farm and the buffalo is preferred to the cow for milk.

Conservation of volume by displacement method

Volume I. This experiment was in two parts. The first part of the experiment, referred to as Volume I in subsequent chapters, was planned to find out whether the boys understand that the volume of an object remains the same irrespective of changes in shape.

Two equal sized balls of plasticine and two glass jars of water were used. The water levels (which were equal in both the jars) were marked by rubber bands. The experimenter then asked the subjects if the two balls were of the same size; if they agreed the experiment was resumed, otherwise they were asked to make the two balls the same size. The subject was given one of the balls, a painted bamboo stick and one of the glass jars of water. The experimenter used the other set of equipment. Then the experimenter immersed his ball in the water and asked the subject to do the same with his ball. The new levels of water were marked by adjusting rubber bands. When the subject agreed that the two balls displaced the same amount of water in the two jars, the experimenter removed his ball and rolled it into a sausage shape (in front of the child) and asked the following question: 'If I put this sausage completely in this jar (pointing) would the water come up to the same level as before or to a higher or a lower level?' When the subject had finished answering the question he was asked the reason for his response: 'Why do you think so?' Some of the boys changed their minds after offering an explanation; they were then asked to give further explanation for their answers.

Volume II. In the second part of the experiment the subject was asked to compare the weight by 'feel' of a ping pong ball and a ball of plasticine of the same size. (The plasticine ball was prepared before the experiment to ensure equal volumes.) When the child was fully satisfied that the two balls were of the same size but different weights, the plasticine ball was immersed in water and the new level marked with a rubber band. The ball was taken out and put aside on the table, and the subjects were asked the following question: 'If I push this (pointing) ping pong ball completely into the water — would the water rise to the same level as before or higher or lower?' The subject was asked the reason for his answer. Their understanding of this process (that volume is related to occupied space rather than weight) was further tested by asking them the following question: 'If I take a lead ball, which is of equal size to the plasticine ball, and put it fully into the water, would the level of the water rise to the same level as with the plasticine ball or a higher or lower level?' Again reasons for the responses were asked. Because of the problem of possible development of a response-set, this test was not given at the same time as the other Conservation tests of Weight and Area.

Because of the slow pace of working of the Punjabi groups this test was abandoned when testing in Punjab. Much encouragement was needed to get any responses and it was felt that considerations of time, finance and knowledge gained did not warrant extra testing.

Scoring

There is as yet no agreed rationale for scoring the responses of children on Piagetian tests (Greet *et al.*, 1971). The use of ordinal and interval scales by various researchers (e.g. Vernon, 1969) has been based on speculation rather than demonstrable empirical or theoretical considerations. In view of the above mentioned difficulty, it was decided to use a nominal scale for each test and not to add up subjects' marks on conservation tests as such. Thus a score of 1 was awarded to conservers and '0' to the non-conservers in each of the tests and the scores treated separately for analysis. The subjects who wavered in their responses between conservers and non-conservers were classified as non-conservers. In the Volume II test the subjects who gave correct answers to only one of the problems were classified as C/NC. Thus we had three categories to record subjects' answers: Conservers, C/NC and Non Conservers.

Equivalence test (card-sorting test)

It was mentioned in the previous section that notions of concepts can be based either on the premise of variability within things or on the premise of variability between things. Conservation problems are based on the former, whereas the studies of concept formation are based on the latter notion. To categorize, according to Bruner (1967b, p. 1): '. . . is to render discriminably different things equivalent, to group the objects and events and people around us into classes, and to respond to them in terms of their class membership rather than their uniqueness.' He further argues that categories for grouping objects and events are invented by man to simplify his environment.

It can be argued that man in all societies, communities and tribes has used categories to make sense of the bewildering varieties of things. Through the use of categories man can adapt himself to his surroundings easily both by simplifying the complexity of the environment and by reducing the necessity to learn everything *de novo*. However, the nature and kind of categories used by individuals depends on the language, cultural artefacts, myths and folklore of the society. Of these, language is by far the most important instrument of categorization. Thus Whorf wrote (1956, p. 28): '. . . we dissect nature along lines laid by our native language. The categories and types that we isolate from the world of phenomena we do not find because they stare every observer in the face; on the contrary, the world is presented in a kaleidoscopic flux of impressions which has to be organized by our minds. We cut nature up, organize it into concepts, and ascribe significance as we do largely because we are party to an agreement to organize it in this way . . .'

In view of the importance of this psychological process and the fact that a study probing the bases of equivalence groupings would complement the study of conservation ability, the card-sorting test was included in the battery. Olver and Hornsby (1967) have devised and used a test to investigate the bases of children's grouping behaviour. A modified version of this was successfully used by Davey (1968) in this country to assess the abilities of Tristan da Cunha children. The test consists of 42 pictures of things in everyday use, including items relating to clothing, tools, transport vehicles, animals and plants. This test was adapted for use in this study, so that objects used in the test were not entirely unfamiliar to the boys. (The full list of things used in the research appear in the Appendix B). However, in this test 42 objects were drawn in water colours on cards (3½" x 2½") by an artist in an appealing manner. As the purpose of the study was to compare the performance of boys brought up in different social milieux, it was decided to use the same set of drawings in England and in Punjab. The basic principle determining the choice of objects for drawing was that all the boys should have prior knowledge of the objects; however, this had to be sacrificed in a few instances as it was not always possible to include objects which were equally familiar to the three groups of boys. For instance, the boys in Punjab were more familiar with such objects as a buffalo, a pumpkin and a waterpump; whereas boys in this country had more experience of things like cars, garages and aeroplanes. The choice of the objects was vindicated as only a few boys failed to recognize them.

The drawings were spread on a table in a pre-planned sequence to randomize the colour, shape, function etc., of the objects. The boys were asked to go through the pictures and make sure they knew all the objects; and in the case of any drawing(s) not recognized, to ask me. I then adopted a standard procedure of telling them the name of any such objects and giving a brief description of it/them. The following instructions were then given: 'Look through the pictures again and pick out the pictures which you think go together in some way.' If the subjects asked such questions as: 'Is it colour or shape?' they were told to group them 'as you like as long as they go together'. Boys were asked and encouraged to make ten attempts in all. After each trial (or grouping) the boys were asked: 'Why do you think they go together?' The responses were recorded. The pictures were replaced after each trial and the subjects were asked to go on making groups.

Boys in Punjab were given equivalent instructions in Punjabi. These children needed a lot of encouragement and persuasion to make more than five attempts. They were poor in articulation of the reasons for their grouping and a great deal of time was spent in eliciting responses. The responses of the Punjabi boys were recorded by a graduate assistant in the Punjabi language, and a similar record was kept in this country by the author.

In order to analyse the responses, a simplified version of the Olver and Hornsby scheme was used. According to this framework children's groupings can demonstrate both the basis on which objects are considered to be similar and structures of groups. The following scheme was used:

1. Basis of groupings:
   a) Perceptible: colour, shape, size
   b) Functional: use, etc.
   c) Nominal: existing names in language

2. Structure of grouping:
   a) Super-ordinate
   b) Complexive (collection and chain)
   c) Thematic
   d) Fiat

This scheme of classification will be discussed with examples in a subsequent chapter.

Vygotsky blocks

The card-sorting test does not place any constraints on the child; he is free to group objects as he likes as he keeps on giving reasons for his groupings. The examiner has no fixed criteria (criterial attributes) in mind against which the groupings are to be evaluated.

Vygotsky (1962) devised a set of blocks (22 in total) to investigate the various phases through which children's thinking progresses prior to the stage of thinking with true concepts. The test, unlike the card-sorting test discussed earlier, imposes a structure within which children have to respond. Vygotsky describes three major phases through which the child passes before attaining maturity in concept formation: vague syncretic; thinking in complexes; potential concept. During the vague syncretic phase the child's sorting behaviour is influenced by fleeting imagery and consequently his thinking is inconsistent. The blocks are sorted out randomly or grouped on the basis that they are nearer to each other. As the author sums it: 'his thinking is characterized by incoherent coherence'. In the next phase the grouping of blocks is based on perceptual (colour, shape, size) attributes of the blocks, which however, are not abstracted from the contexts. According to Vygotsky: 'In a complex, the bonds between its components are concrete and factual rather than abstract and logical' (Vygotsky, 1962, p. 61). However, in this phase the child is already less egocentric and more objective in his thinking. The third stage described by Vygotsky is named the potential concept phase, in which the child's sorting is based on a definite criterion — unlike the complex stage in which criteria of sorting are vague and diffuse. The criterion, however, is not abstracted from the blocks. In the final stage children can abstract attributes from the practical content and do their sortings systematically. This stage is similar to that of Piaget's stage of formal operations; during which adolescents can formulate and systematically test their hypotheses.

The description of this test is given by its author, Vygotsky (1962, p. 29):

'. . . The material consists of 22 wooden blocks varying in colour, shape, height and size. There are five different colours, six different shapes, two heights (the tall blocks and the flat blocks), and two sizes of the horizontal surface. On the underside of each figure, which is not seen by the subject is written one of the four nonsense words — lag, bik, mur, cev. Regardless of colour or shape, lag is written on all tall large figures, bik on all flat large figures, mur on the tall small ones and cev on the small flat ones.'

The blocks were mixed up and placed on the table in full view of the subjects. They were asked to look at the blocks carefully and the following instructions were given: 'I want you to sort these blocks into four groups. Each group has a name — as there are four groups, there are four different names of the blocks. I will show you an example. This block (large yellow square) has the word "lag" underneath. (Afterwards, this block is placed on the left-hand corner of the table.) You could start by placing the blocks which you think go with this block and then make the other three groups in the other three corners of the table (pointing). You can move the blocks from corner to corner and back to the middle of the table (pointing) if you would like to. Please don't upturn any blocks. I shall help you by turning over wrongly chosen blocks.'

Boys were encouraged to verbalize their thinking whilst sorting. After each sorting they were asked the reasons for their grouping. When the subjects had finished the experiment they were asked the basis on which the final sorting was done. The blocks were upturned and mixed up and the subjects were asked to repeat the sorting; this was considered necessary to ascertain whether the subjects had acquired the concept or were still thinking at a perceptual level.

This experiment was tried on a number of English and British Punjabi boys of 10+ and 11+ age groups to standardize the instruction procedures. Thus we labelled the table as shown in the diagram below:

Subject

2		1
	M	
3		4

Experimenter

Using short forms for the names of the blocks and numbers and arrows to follow the positional moves; it was therefore possible to recreate a given subject's strategies for subsequent analysis.

Scoring

The purpose of the experiment was to look closely at the strategies employed by the subjects when they were obliged to form a concept. However, it was considered that scoring would provide additional data for comparisons of the groups. Semeonoff and Laird (1952) and Semeonoff and Trist (1958) have devised a method of scoring the performance of subjects on Vygotsky Blocks. This scheme takes into consideration both the number of blocks upturned and the quality of the solution. The following equation is used to arrive at the final score:

$$*Score = Time + 5 \text{ (clues)} + 10 \text{ (grade } -1)$$

This test was not given as a speed test but as a power test to assess ability under relaxed conditions, hence the time factor was omitted from the equation. The number of clues, excluding the first block, was counted and a grade of solution was worked out from definitions given by Semeonoff and Trist (1958).

Grade I	Any explanation which takes into account the double dichotomy of size and thickness, or otherwise takes into account the fact that two criteria have to be combined.
Grade II	An imperfect realization of the dichotomy where one of the two criteria is deemed less important than the other. Or a grade III solution amended, on prompting, to what would have been grade I if given spontaneously.
Grade III	a. More or less intuitive apprehension in terms of one element, usually 'size'. Any answer which depends on inter-relationships between groups is a grade III solution.
	b. However adequate an explanation may be in other respects it must be rated as grade III if the subject persists in adding that he tried to work in something else as well, e.g. each colour and each shape represented in each group.
Grade IV	If no explanation, or only a vague one even with prompting, the subject should be asked to re-sort the blocks — if successful, a grade IV solution may be credited, if not, the performance is rated grade V.
Grade V (score 40)	No explanation and wrong re-sorting at the second attempt.

*High scores indicate low performance and vice versa.

WISC Block Design

Koh's Block Design test was originally devised to measure general intelligence through the use of non-verbal material. But subsequent studies (see Macfarlane, 1964) showed that it also measures spatial ability. According to Witkin (1966) tests of this type measure the ability to analyse, abstract and synthesize like the other tests of field-dependence, e.g. figure embedded test. Vernon (1969), Berry (1965) and Dawson (1967) have used Block Design tests of various types in their cross-cultural researches.

The results of a pilot study in this country with a number of English and Punjabi boys showed that Koh's Block Design test was a very time consuming test. Furthermore, most of the designs were found difficult by the boys of this ability range. Therefore it was decided to use a simpler and a shorter test of Block Design; WISC Block Design fulfills these requirements. This is the only speed test included in the battery, and it was hoped that the results would give some indication of the working speed of various groups of boys. The test was given according to the standard instructions (Wechsler, 1949) and the raw scores were converted to standardized scores and used for analyses.

The Coloured Progressive Matrices (A, Ab, B)

This test, according to Raven (1965), is devised 'to assess mental development up to the age when a person is sufficiently able to reason by analogy and to adopt this way of thinking as a consistent method of inference.' It is suggested by Raven that the test itself is not a test of general intelligence and should not be used as such. However, it has been shown that the scores from this test do indicate general ability (Vernon, 1969).

This test was given as a group test to all the samples, according to the standard instructions (Raven, 1965). The boys in Punjab were given the test in small groups (five to seven) to maintain close and personal contact as the boys had no experience in taking tests of this kind. The raw scores were used for analysis as a number of boys were older than 11 years, and norms are not given above this age level.

At this point it is appropriate to make a case for the use of this test with the boys over the age of 11, as the standard Progressive Matrices test (i.e. C, D and E) is considered to be more suitable for this age group. The decision to use this version was based on the knowledge that the boys in Punjab have no experience with this type of material and would find the sets C, D and E extremely difficult. This stance was vindicated by the results, as will be seen in the following chapters. As this study is a comparative one, it was thought best to use the same version with the groups in this country.

Goodenough-Harris Draw-a-man test

This test is usually given to assess children's intellectual maturity (Harris, 1963), where other measures, e.g. verbal tests, are considered inappropriate. Veronon (1969, p. 143) has used this test in his researches and suggests that the test provides additional information on perceptual-spatial ability. The test was given and scored according to the manual. Due to shortage of time this test was not given to boys in Punjab. Anyway, it is doubtful whether their responses to this test would have been reliable and valid as their drawing and sketching skills are so poor.

Ability and attitudes ratings

The tests described so far top the basic psychological processes of thinking and are not as such measurement of attainment in any of the school subjects. It was considered important to compare the abilities of the English and the British Punjabi boys, which are explicitly developed through school teaching. The use of standardized tests in the two basic subjects (English and arithmetic) had to be reluctantly given up as the boys were already asked to devote a substantial amount of their time to the research.

The class teachers were asked to rate the boys on a five-point scale. It was suggested that, as far as possible, they should place 10 per cent of children in category A and E; 20 per cent in categories B and D and 40 per cent in category C. The following abilities and attitudes were rated by the class teachers:

1. Abilities —
   - (a) Spoken English
   - (b) Written English
   - (c) Comprehension
   - (d) Arithmetic
2. Attitudes —
   - (a) Boys attitude towards school and learning
   - (b) Parents' attitude to school and 'Education'
   - (c) The class teachers were also requested to rate the boys on degree of participation in non-academic school activities such as school plays, games and outings.

The teachers' rating of children's abilities are often less reliable and valid as compared with the standardized tests; however, their perceptions of pupils have considerable predictive and educational value. Haynes (1971) found that ability ratings given by the teachers were good predictors of performance on the Staffordshire Arithmetic test and on the Holborn Comprehensive Scale.

Semi-structured interview

Researches of Griffiths (1971), Craft (1970), Bernstein (1971) and Douglas (1964) have clearly shown the importance of home background factors on scholastic achievement. The contribution of family can be mapped along four major dimensions: the authority structure and patterns of sanctions within the family; the socio-cultural quality of the home; the degree to which the child is exposed to educational activities and learning facilities; and finally, whether or not parents perceive education as being a worthwhile and desirable experience and one which merits their support.

The Punjabi immigrants come from a traditional culture (which we shall describe in detail in the next chapter) with different value systems from those of the English. Consequently, it was thought desirable to investigate the degree to which they have adopted the norms and values of the English Society — especially on the above mentioned dimensions. It was hoped that such an investigation would enable us to comment meaningfully on the nature of the contribution which such immigrant homes might, or might not, be making to the intellectual development of their boys.

The use of a questionnaire or an attitude scale was ruled out because no such reliable instrument was available. It was felt prudent to probe such an area by a face-to-face semi-structured interview conducted bilingually (English/Punjabi), which would also help to overcome a further problem facing a questionnaire, namely, the linguistic deficiencies of many of the boys in the sample. The following areas were explored: (1) Use of the English language in the home; (2) General activities reflecting the adoption of English norms and interaction with the host culture; (3) Adherence to Punjabi culture; (4) Educational experiences provided by the families.

The first category consisted of such items as:

What language do you speak with your parents?
  — with your brothers and sisters?
Does your father take a daily paper?
An Indian or an English one?

Items reflecting the acculturation of the families were on these lines:

Do you go to English pictures? — homes?
What sort of food do you have at home?
Do English people visit you?

To investigate the degree of adherence to Punjabi culture items such as the following were included:

Do you go to a Punjabi school? (i.e. at week-ends)
Does your father go to Gurdawara? (i.e. Sikh temple)
Do your uncles and aunts live in your house?

Finally, the questions in the fourth category went as follows:
Do you have jig-saws or a tool-kit at home?
How many books do you have at home?
Do you use the local library?

For full details of the items on which the interview was based — see Appendix B.

All the boys were interviewed individually (15—20 minutes) and their responses were recorded on the questionnaire for later analysis.

A note on testing of boys in the Punjab and England

A special trip was planned in August 1970 to test the children in Punjab; during my stay, I had to have the help of a Punjabi graduate to transcribe the answers of the children. There was little problem in getting to know the boys and teachers from the two villages as I was brought up- and schooled in one of the villages and have maintained contact with my family and village. I spent a week in both schools prior to testing. During this time I made friends with the children, and also discussed the nature and purpose of the research and the test with the teacher. All the tests were given in the Punjabi language and similarly the answers were recorded in Punjabi. The testing sessions were held in quiet places; generally in the courtyard under a shady tree. The testing was in the following order: (1) Equivalence test; (2) Conservation of Weight and Volume; (3) Raven Matrices; (4) WISC Block Design; (5) Vygotsky Blocks.

The testing in this country was done during the months of May, June and July in 1972. The headmasters were most cooperative and considerate; all of them offered a separate room for testing. In two cases the headmasters allowed the use of their own rooms at considerable inconvenience to themselves. The tests were given the following order: (1) Equivalence test and Conservation tests of Weight and Area; (2) WISC Block Design and Conservation of Volume; (3) Vygotsky Blocks; (4) Home-background interview; (5) Raven Matrices and Draw-a-Man.

Summary

Before I present my hypotheses for the research, a summary of this chapter is considered necessary in view of its length. Matched samples of boys from three cultural groups, Punjabi, British Punjabi and English, were given tests of conservation of Weight and Area, an equivalence test, Vygotsky blocks to test concept formation, Raven matrices, and WISC Block Design. In addition, the samples in England were tested on Draw-a-Man and Conservation of volume tests. The home-background of the British Punjabi was assessed by personal interviews.

The following hypotheses were tested:

1. The British Punjabi boys of age group nine years, nine months to 11 years, ten months are significantly superior to the matched group of indigenous Punjabi boys on (a) WISC Block Design; (b) Raven Matrices; (c) Vygotsky Block; (d) Conservation of Weight and Area; (e) Equivalence test.
2. The performance of the senior boys (11 plus) of three cultural groups is different from the respective junior boys (nine years, nine months plus) on the above mentioned tests.

The following questions were posed:

1. Does the performance of the British Punjabi boys (nine years, nine months to 11 years, ten months) differ significantly from the English boys of the same age range on the above mentioned tests?
2. Do the abilities and attitudes of British Punjabi boys, as rated by the teachers, differ significantly from those of the English boys of the same age group?

Social and Educational Background of the Punjabis

A majority of the immigrants from India are Punjabis and of these a very large number come from four districts of Punjab: Jullundur, Hoshiarpur, Ludhiana and Amritsar. These districts contain hundreds of villages which are poorly connected to the main towns. The main access from these villages to towns is by dust tracks (recently some have been connected by concrete roads), and the main transport is by bullock cart or bicycles. Life in the villages has always been very hard; farmers have toiled day and night and throughout the year to make a reasonable living. There are no holidays, no weekends and no rest periods on the farm, except for occasional religious festivals. Farmers own very small farms — the large majority have holdings below 15 acres. The farmers, until recently, have depended on rain, cow dung and well tried seeds to grow their crops, and as a consequence barely made a living from their farms. However, the government has recently been successful in persuading them, especially the big landlords, to use new varieties of seeds, install tube-wells or use canal water and to apply chemical fertilizers. As a result the production has gone up; but as we know, this has led to further problems, e.g. scarcity of chemicals and inability to pay the world price.

The villages are mainly inhabited by farmers and Harijans — the lowest caste in India, who provide almost all the labour for the farmers. Also there are a few artisans in each village, e.g. a carpenter, a blacksmith, who provide services to the farmers, and who are mostly paid in kind for their work.

Traditionally, these areas of Punjab have provided a large number of recruits for the Indian Army. This is mainly due to the fact that life on the farms, as indicated, was hard and unrewarding; whereas there was a promise of better living conditions and financial rewards in the army. The Sikhs are well known for their courage and valour and still form the backbone of the Indian Army.

The other escape route for the dissatisfied has been through emigration. For generations, farmers have sought their fortunes in countries like Canada, Kenya and Malaysia, and more recently in Britain. The large-scale emigration to Britain, in the '60s, has largely been due to the employment opportunities, good wages and good living standards. I think it is worth noting here that all the immigrants from these areas were not illiterate farmers, but included a high proportion of graduates who were either unemployed or were attracted by the high wages and the prospect of travel.

The Punjabis in Britain have sent a great deal of money back to their families and relatives who in turn have improved their living standards; new brick-built houses have replaced the old mud houses; tractors and tube-wells have replaced the bullocks and the Persian wheels. All round there has been an improvement. The sample of Punjabi boys for our study were taken from two villages which are in Jullundur district, and it is within this social context that we have to interpret the results of our research.

Religion

Sikhism, the religion of the inhabitants of these areas, and of the majority of the Punjabi immigrants, was founded by Guru Nanak who lived from 1469 AD to 1539 AD. The principles of this religion were the results of synthesis of Hindu and Muslim theologies and beliefs, and are to be found in the sacred books of the Sikhs — Adi Granth. The basic teaching may be summarized as follows: belief in one God, emphasis on pure and simple life, and belief in non-violence. This religion was embraced mostly by the Hindus who were tired of superstitions and cults, and were disgusted with the practices of the Brahmins (priests), who had exploited the masses for their own welfare. All in all there were nine other Gurus, who preached the basic teachings of Nanak, and who also made contributions to the theology and literature of the Sikh religion. Guru Gobind Singh, the tenth and the last Guru, introduced the fundamental changes in the religion to meet the challenge of the new social and political order. During this period, India was ruled by Aurangzeb (a Moghul ruler), who was a fanatic Muslim. His policy of repression and Jihad (conversion of Hindus to Islam) aroused great indignation amongst the spiritual leadership of the Hindus and Sikh communities. It was in response to this policy of repression that Guru Gobind Singh actively armed the Sikhs and welded them into a well disciplined para-military force to fight against the injustices of the Moghul rulers. His soldiers were supposed to keep their hair long (kesh) — hence the reluctance shown by some Sikhs in this country to cut their hair and replace turbans by caps; keep a comb to keep their hair clean (*kanga*); to wear special shorts (*kaeshara*), to keep a sword for protection (*karpan*) and wear an iron bangle (*kara*). These are known as the five 'Ks' of the Sikhs. They were also forbidden to smoke tobacco or marijuana and were not to use drugs of any sort. He also preached and practised the importance of fellowship. He introduced a new dimension to the religion, so that its followers could face up to the challenges of the then contemporary society. These values and symbols have been passed on from generation to generation and have given the Sikh community a homogeneity and an identity unique among the people of India, and this group solidarity extends to all Sikh communities found outside Punjab.

The Gurdawara (Sikh temple) is the central place in most of the villages. People assemble once a month to worship, to socialize and to talk about local and national politics. The Gurdawara plays an important part in the life of the Sikhs: this is the place where new babies are baptised, marriage ceremonies are performed and last prayers are said for the dead. Indeed, all the significant occasions connected with the community are celebrated here: Indeed, the Gurdawara performs the same functions as the Church did in this country until recent times. It is because of this tradition that we find Gurdawaras in cities and towns wherever there is a sizeable population of Punjabi Sikhs.

Social system and values

The Punjabis have a strong tradition of extended family, and it would be rare indeed to find a couple living on their own in a village. A typical household would include grandparents, sons and their wives, and their children. The number of people living in one household could be as many as 20. This communal living, in my view, is in response both to the working conditions and the nature of farms. This unity of family is necessary in view of the fact that the farms require an abundant supply of labour during the sowing and harvesting time in order to make the most of opportune weather conditions. However, these farms have been handed down from generation to generation and consequently have become smaller and smaller — in some cases reduced to only a couple of acres. Any further attempt to sub-divide the property is strongly resisted by the head of the household.

This type of communal living necessitates collective thinking and action, and individuality of any sort is actively discouraged. An adolescent or a young man who is obedient, works day and night and never questions the authority of the elders is universally praised and admired. Equally, the erring young man who breaks the social conventions and 'rocks the boat' elicits universal condemnation. Quite often, awkward young men are quickly married off, in the hope that the added responsibility will bring them back into the social fold.

Almost all the marriages are arranged by the family; the young man or woman has no say in the matter. It is the responsibility of the family to find a suitable spouse, and this is generally based on considerations of caste, religion, wealth, status and social prestige. Of these, caste and religion are probably the most important. Very few marriages are arranged outside the community. This tradition, in my view, explains the hesitation of many Punjabi parents in this country to send their children, especially girls, to mixed schools. Similarly, the reluctance of Punjabi parents to allow their adolescent boys and girls to go to youth clubs is based on misgivings that they might marry outside the community.

Dowry is invariably given by the bride's parents and sometimes it might run into thousands of rupees (£1 = 18Rs approx.). This custom has become so rooted in the system that some parents are obliged to spend the whole of their life's savings on their daughters' marriages. While most parents in Europe do indeed help their children in whatever financial ways they can, in India, this sensible and practical custom has been exploited by selfish people and has become a rigid bargaining practice and a great burden to parents of mainly girl families. This is the reason why Punjabis prefer boys to girls and it explains why the upbringing of the boys is so different from that of the girls. My experience suggests that in Britain, this social practice, far from beginning to weaken as it is in India, is becoming more widespread, more rigidly adhered to, and more expensive. Indeed, almost all the Punjabi immigrants in this country follow this wretched custom and consequently exhaust all their savings on the weddings. I have attended weddings in which household goods and jewellery costing hundreds of pounds along with a house and money to buy a car were given to the bridegroom and his family.

The roles of men and women are clearly separated and strongly adhered to. Generally, men work on the farms and look after the affairs of the family, whereas women are in charge of the household affairs including the rearing of children. Men and women have separate circles of friends and no social mixing of the two sexes ever takes place. Whereas men usually gossip with their friends about crops, local politics and weather conditions, women gossip and moan amongst themselves about their mothers-in-law, husbands and children. The use of alcohol is quite common amongst men, and as a matter of fact, because of its frequent use, it is considered to be the cause of most of the village quarrels. Women, by tradition, never touch alcoholic drinks, and this explains the fact that Punjabi women never accompany their husband to the pubs in this country. Married women practice purdah — which is a custom of covering the face with the headscarf in the presence of men who are older than their husband. However, this custom is seldom practised by the women in this country.

The two important institutions of the village, the Gurdawara and Panchayat (assembly) are run by the men. Women are not barred from holding office; indeed, on some occassions they have been elected as heads of the village assemblies. The Panchayats play an important role in the social and political life of the villages. The office-bearers are elected by the villages under the supervision of the local government officers and hold office for three years. This body has executive as well as judicial functions. It hears cases of local disputes and has legal powers to boycott and to impose a fine on the guilty party. However, its main function is to act as a conciliator between the parties, and the office-bearers use their influence to patch up quarrels and settle other issues without formal meetings.

The morality and world-view of the villagers is largely based on the Sikh religion which preaches, amongst other virtues, the values of hard work, brotherhood and fellowship. However, in practice the followers fall far short of this morality which is true of followers of all religions. Quarrelling and fighting within the families and between the families is endemic in villages and dissipates a lot of their energies and resources. Indeed, some of the family and kinship feuds are so persistent that they are pursued with vigour even in this country. But it should also be noted that Punjabis do work hard, both in their native country and overseas. In this country they are well known both for the long hours they put into their jobs and for their capacity to stick to hard jobs, e.g. the hot and filthy jobs in foundries.

Regarding their world-view, the Sikhs believe in one God, whom they regard as the creator of the universe. The nature of man, according to them, is a mixture of good and bad, and it is up to man to redeem himself through his own efforts. On this theological issue, Sikhs differ from the Hindu concept of *Karma* (that the deeds of the past life determine the quality of the present). The passionate believers in *Karma* often adopt a fatalistic attitude to life — which incidentally has been the psychological handicap to progress of large sections of Indians. Sikhs, with their belief in the virtue of man's effort, have been only too ready to try to improve their standard of living, particularly by emigration.

The caste system is very much a part of the Indian way of life. This is endemic in all communities, regions and provinces of India. It was devised by Manu (see Nehru, 1947), an Indian political philosopher, to streamline the functions of society. *Brahmins*, the highest caste, were to engage in spiritual, political and scholarly matters; *Kashatriya* were to act as military guardians of the society; *Vaish* were to engage in farming and trading and, finally, *Shudras* — who were later treated as

untouchables — were to serve the other three castes. The caste of the
person came to be decided upon by his birth rather than by his
achievement and personal virtue. In some ways, the system is similar to
that of Plato, who strongly argued for the stratification of men's
positions into golden, silver and iron categories.

Sikhs were forbidden by their gurus to practice the caste system:
whereas the Hindus barred the lowest caste (*Harijan*) from their temples
and forbade them to read the sacred books, the Gurus included the
hymns and thoughts of eminent *Shudras (Harijan)* in their religious
books. Anyone, irrespective of his caste, according to guru Gobind
Singh, could become a *Khalsa* (pure person) and consequently a worthy
member of the Sikh community. However, the society was so saturated
with the idea and practice of caste that it soon affected the outlook of
almost all Sikhs. Although they do not bar the *Shudras* from their
Gurudwaras, there is very little social mixing, and mixed marriages are
extremely rare.

Education in Punjab

The development of mass education did not gain momentum until
well after the independence of India in 1947. Before this time, only a
handful of well-off parents could afford to send their children even to
primary schools. For the majority of villagers, children were of great
help in doing chores both on the farms and in the homes and
consequently, they were considered to be great economic assets.
Moreover, schools were not available in each and every village, and the
vast majority of school-going children had to travel miles to attend
primary schools. These long journeys, especially on hot dusty roads,
were a great obstacle to the spread of primary education. During this
time the education of girls in the villages was non-existent. A very small
number of progressive parents sent their daughters to attend separate
schools for girls but the vast majority of girls were illiterate, though a
small proportion learnt to read and write Punjabi in the village
Gurdawara.

However, major changes have taken place in the sphere of education
since 1947. Primary education is free, and the government has made
tremendous efforts to establish schools in all large villages, and as a
result the vast majority of the children now go to their own local
schools. Although primary education is compulsory, it is rarely
enforced, especially in remote villages. So even today a number of
children in the villages do not attend primary schools to acquire the
basic skills of reading and writing.

Whilst the policy of free primary education has been well implemen-
ted, the situation regarding secondary education is far less satisfactory.
Secondary education is neither free nor compulsory, and as a result the

poorer sections of the community cannot afford to send their children to high schools. Moreover, high schools are not easily accessible to large numbers of villages, and long journeys in winter and in hot summers are still the chief obstacle to the spread of secondary education. Most of the high schools are run by religious bodies such as Khalsa Panth, Arya *mandals* and Hindu *sabas*, and the role of the government is chiefly confined to 'filling in the gaps'.

As the schools receive only a small grant from the government and have to rely chiefly on tuition fees, there is often intense competition amongst the schools to attract the maximum number of students. As a consequence classes are usually large (45+) and teachers often resort to drill methods of teaching. However, there are no discipline problems as only the well motivated and the willing join the schools. The success of these schools is entirely judged by the number of students obtaining good passes in the matriculation examination (roughly equivalent to O—levels) of the local universities. There is tremendous pressure on teachers to produce results as, for example, a number of school managers operate 'payment by result' schemes. Such a system has restricted both the development of general education and of aesthetic subjects such as drama, art and music.

Most of the high school matriculates either takes up clerical jobs or go to teachers' colleges to be trained as primary school teachers. Only a small proportion go to universities or colleges to study for a degree. The failure rate in degree examinations is very high (30 per cent plus) for a variety of reasons, e.g. large classes, poor facilities for studies. The successful candidates have high aspirations but the majority have to accept low-paid clerical jobs or resort to teaching which is not very well rewarded either. This probably explains why so many Punjabi graduates have emigrated to this country to seek their fortunes.

Our major interest in this chapter, however, lies with the village primary schools, which provided the samples for this research. The primary school is often situated outside the village and consists of three to four rooms and a big yard or school compound where the children can play. In the yard there are invariably big shady trees under which classes are held, especially during the hot summer days. In winter too, the classes are often taught outside in the sun. During the winter months flowers like marigolds are grown in abundance around the school, but grass which is so popular in England is rarely grown in Punjab as it requires a lot of water during the summer months. The main source of water in schools is a hand waterpump which supplies water for drinking, washing and for the flowers. There are no toilets as such and calls of nature are usually answered in the surrounding fields.

Primary schools are mixed, but there is a preponderance of boys in the classes because the poor families often keep their girls at home as they have to act as nannies for their younger brothers and sisters. In addition, parents are afraid to break the traditional custom which stresses the virtue of training girls for their future role under the supervision of the mother. The average size of the school is 150, and there are generally three teachers to cater for this number of pupils. Almost all the teachers are from the basic training colleges and quite a number of them are women. The pay of the teachers is not very high and a number of them supplement their income by looking after the post office which is often located in the school. Another way of increasing their incomes is by private tutoring, but there is little demand in villages for this type of work because of the meagre resources of the villagers. Quite a number of teachers get seasonal farm produce from the villagers in return for small favours, such as letter writing and form filling.

Schools by and large are poorly equipped; for example, there are few visual aids, charts, diagrams and other illustrative material and no audiovisual equipment. The only aid to which teachers have ready access is the blackboard. However, the children's books are written interestingly and have colourful pictures and other illustrative material. The subjects which receive most of the time are the 3 Rs; only a small proportion of time is devoted to other subjects such as geography, history and general science. Furthermore, teachers ignore the indigenous forms of thought and modes of experiences which are enshrined in folk poetry, drama, myth and religious texts. As a result, the curricula of these schools is often very narrow and rigid.

The relationship between the children and the teacher is based on the traditional concept of Guru—Chaela (master-disciple), which is reflected in the seating arrangement of the pupils. Whereas teachers use chairs, children have to sit on the mats or on the bare ground or floor. No doubt scarce resources are partly responsible for this situation, but this is a constant reminder to the children of their inferior status. Children invariably respect their teachers and are always willing to submit to their superior wisdom. They are extremely obedient, and seldom question their teachers even on academic matters, as it is considered extremely rude to do so. This form of relationship makes the job of the teacher easy in a way, as he relies on imparting information and facts through the most formal method and avoids questions, discussions and debates.

Children learn their tables, methods of doing sums and other facts and information by rote. There is rarely a deep understanding of the concepts involved in the school work. In my view the reasons for this excessive reliance on memory may be due to the fact that children do their class work on slates and *phatis* (a rectangular wooden strip with a coating of clay for practising spelling and writing dictation), and have no access to their previous work as they have continually to erase their sums and writing from slates and *phatis*. Thus children are denied both the opportunity to learn from their own work and to revise rules of addition, subtractions, etc., and consequently resort to learning everything by rote.

This might also explain the poor motivation of children in these schools, as they have no access to their previous work. My personal experience of this type of schooling was confirmed during my research in 1970. Questions probing the reasons in conservation tasks met with dumb silences, and a lot of prompting and encouragement was necessary before the children felt confident enough to give any answers.

Children are seldom provided with first-hand experience on which they can base their understanding. Simple, basic work such as sorting and counting of objects and playing with blocks or jigsaws is rarely undertaken. Obviously this lack of experience reinforces the rote learning strategies of the children. For instance, every afternoon there is a chanting of tables for an hour or so, and children are remarkably skillful in applying their skills to computational problems.

Although children respect their teachers and are generally very well behaved, teachers still use harsh methods of disciplining them. Much of the punishment meted out stems from the children's inability to do the school work. An example of this occurred whilst I was conducting my research; a teacher caned the whole class of nine-year-olds because they could not do an addition sum. Furthermore, those teachers who are unsure of themselves in this easy classroom situation utilize a variety of humiliating punishments to ensure accurate rote learning and total obedience. However, the younger teachers are less harsh than the older ones in this respect.

In view of the strong authoritarian attitude of the teachers to the children, it is hardly surprising that individuality of any sort is vehemently curbed. Personal interpretation of facts, flexible approach to problems and novelty in thinking is thus denied to most of the village children. Of course, in this respect, teachers are only following the general ethos of Punjabi society which denies the values of individuality and personal initiative and emphasizes conformity and collective responsibility.

Child-rearing practices

Before we discuss the results of the study of child-rearing practics of Punjabis in Nottingham, a brief outline of these practices in Punjab would provide an interesting and useful background. These observations are based on my personal knowledge and experience, as no definite study of this type as has been published.

To Punjabi families, having babies is the normal and natural way of life and extra preparation, debate and discussion on babyhood and childhood is not considered necessary. This is in sharp contrast to the present day English family, particularly the so-called middle class. The pressures of popular psychology such as in the advice columns in most magazines and newspapers, radio and television programmes regarding the 'normal' or 'average' child's development, make the bringing-up of children in England problematic. Such pressures do not exist in India; mothercraft is acquired from the young mother's family to whom she returns for the birth of the first child. She then stays with her own family for about six months after the birth, and her mother plays a considerable role in shaping her behaviour towards the baby in the traditional way. The new-born baby is kept very close to its mother for comfort and she has plenty of time to devote to the baby's needs. The supportive atmosphere of the extended family is very beneficial to the formation of a good relationship between mother and baby. Feeding is always on demand and breast-feeding is almost universal, although bottle-feeding is creeping in, because of its prestigious association with more wealthy families. Getting the baby to sleep is no problem, because babies always sleep with the mother, and just fall asleep when they feel like it. There are no commercially-made nappies; babies wear a cotton home-made nappy and no rubber pants. Mothers do toilet-train their children, but do not regard it as a problem at all, merely holding the baby out regularly until it performs! All aspects of child-rearing are considered natural and in the extended family even the first child interacts with peers rather than with adults as they have to do in a nuclear family.

Boys are preferred to girls, for reasons that were indicated earlier in this chapter, to the extent that in some families women who have girls are regarded as inadequate and boys are continually given preferential treatment. The role-model for boys is the grandfather, rather than the father who has very little to do with babies and young children; the grandfather is very indulgent to the child until he is displaced by a younger child. Babies are, though, indulged by all the adults and regarded as playthings to entertain. There are no rules of upbringing, mainly because the women can't agree on a 'policy' amongst themselves! All this is not to say that the extended family is heaven for young mothers. The presence of several generations of women in the same house-hold leads to arguments and friction and many individualistic or independent Punjabi women in Britain have told me that they are glad to be free to do as they like without parental interference. But on the whole the extended family does provide tremendous support, particularly to mothers who are in any way inadequate or who have a large family.

When babies start to eat adult food, which is from two to three years of age, they start with natural yogurt, chappatis and mild curry. They also eat homemade biscuits and raw sugar, and occasionally some sweet-meats. Babies are constantly exposed to infection from flies and poor hygiene and are generally lethargic and in poor health, suffering mostly from all kinds of gastro-intestinal disorders and ear, nose, eye and throat infections. Those children who survive and build up immunity during the first four or five years are only infrequently ill after that.

Children are expected to conform and to be utterly obedient from the age of about five onwards. Physical punishment, slapping and hard smacking, is used a lot to this end, the motto being 'spare the rod and spoil the child'. Any form of individuality is actively discouraged, and to this end any defiant or 'negative' aspects of the child's personality are highlighted and nicknamed until they disappear. Ridicule and sarcasm are frequently-used weapons. The children must not argue with adults, even when they could be right — a special docility which is widely noticed and remarked upon by teachers here. It is not what is said, but *who* says it, that is important. 'I think' or 'I like' does not come into a Punjabi child's vocabulary. Indian teachers here have remarked to me that they have been surprised by the number of times English children express their own opinion. Children in India respect the whole village; all children are known to all adults and they can be corrected or reprimanded by anyone. On the other hand, one must say that these Punjabi children have so many people to relate to affectionately and warmly in the extended family, that they have the utmost emotional security and child neglect or child cruelty or battering is completely unknown. Children are extremely attached to their mother, much more than to their fathers, since he takes very little part in rearing them. In fact, he is kept aloof as the ultimate authority on misdemeanours. The male figure of affection is the grandfather, and this observation may explain something that has been a great mystery to British people — that is, the apparently heartless ease with which large numbers of Punjabi fathers were able to leave their families behind when they came to work in England. Often it was eight years of more before they joined him after he had worked and saved and bought a house here.

From the beginning, children have few toys other than a rattle or a small doll, and no books. They play mostly with things lying about on the ground and household objects and have no experience of manipulative toys of any kind. From infanthood the language used is very much in the style of the limited, contextual restricted code, akin to that described by Bernstein. Happenings are not explained in any way — these factors may explain the poor perceptual development of Punjabi children.

When they are not at school children mostly play outside and occupying their leisure time presents adults with no problems. As I have mentioned before, all the aspects of British children's upbringing which are regarded as a problem such as behaviour, eating, sleeping, are all just a matter of course to Indian parents. In fact, the only problem which regularly appears is the question of the dowry; because of it, from the earliest age girls are a constant worry and the father of several girls may often, indeed, think his life is finished in his 20s when faced with saving tens of thousands of rupees for the dowries.

There are few occasions when there is any celebration for the children to participate in: their birthdays are, if celebrated at all, marked by a religious ceremony and a party for adults. Music, art, dancing and singing are regarded as feminine pursuits, if encouraged at all, toughness being the virtue most admired in boys. Therefore, some of the special occasions most enjoyed and remembered by Punjabi boys and girls are the long winter evenings when their grandfather told them enchanting stories of the Indian past and heritage as they sat all around him learning the greatest legends from various religious texts, not only from their own.

It may appear to the European reader that life for the young Punjabi child must be dull and arid without all the toys which are taken for granted here. However, when one observes the great determination with which the Sikh immigrants apply themselves to whatever job is available, however menial, and the great courage and coolness with which the first generation immigrant faces up to the many problems from a totally different culture, one can only conclude that this stable, warm, loving childhood gives a person a tremendous inner strength and calm which is helping to keep the present-day immigrant families intact in spite of outside cultural pressures.

Child-rearing study in Nottingham

It is now widely recognized that child rearing-practices are important not only to the social and emotional adjustment of children in school, but also to their intellectual development and styles of learning. For example, Bernstein and his colleagues (1971) have illustrated how the speech codes acquired by children in the family affect their subsequent learning and performance, and studies of Witkin and his corroborators, which were reviewed in Chapter 2, have clearly demonstrated how the early training in independence, and experience with perceptual material, orientates the child towards becoming field-independent, i.e. inquiring and perceiving further than the simple explanation. In view of the theoretical importance of such studies, and of the many requests from colleagues both in schools and colleges of education, I decided to undertake some field work among Punjabi families living in this country. This resulting pilot-study is mainly descriptive, having no deep theoretical basis; its primary aim is to discover whether the pattern of child-rearing, as described earlier, has changed.

It is extremely difficult to interview Punjabi women about these personal aspects of family life, particularly for a man, so the study was done in Nottingham where my sister lives, and she was able to accompany me to all of the homes. The sample consisted of 32 Punjabi families having one or more children between the ages of six months and 3½ years, living in the inner-city area and occupying their own houses. It was not a random sample; on the contrary, it was deliberately chosen through friends and relatives to ensure a friendly atmosphere. Random sampling in such a study would not have given valid results, since even in this case, where the families were known to me, one interview had to be discontinued because of hostility engendered by questions which were considered too personal.

The interview was semi-structured in a very informal atmosphere with each individual family. After the usual courtesies and cups of tea with Indian sweetmeats, the purpose of the interview was explained. A tape recorder was tried out but completely ruined the spontaneity of the interview so the idea was abandoned and responses recorded discreetly by symbols on paper. There were no fixed questions, only topics from which the relevant responses were picked out. The conversation often wandered back and forth between Indian ways and their present situation. On the whole, the mothers were extremely eager to to contrast and compare the two systems. In particular, they thought that children have such a favoured and healthy babyhood here, with all the necessary things readily available, easy access to doctor and nurse and remedies and with their mothers having so much more time to look after them as a result of having household appliances, unlike India where, after the baby is a few months old, the mother is fully occupied with very time-consuming cooking. Mothers also felt pleased that they are able to buy all the things their children need, because of the reasonable wages here; however, the needs are felt to be more in the line of clothes and such like rather than toys and books.

It was decided to concentrate on the following aspects of the family during the interview: the structure of the family and parental education and occupation; children's feeding and sleeping patterns; mother's attitude to toilet-training, discipline, permissiveness; provision of toys and learning experiences; independence training; use of mother substitutes and father's participation in the child's daily routine. Incidentally, most families had more than one child on which to base their experience and 12 of them were large, with 4 or more children. In all 32 families the father worked in a semi-skilled or unskilled job, although 30 per cent had a university education and prior to emigration were teachers, while another 30 per cent were clerks and the remaining 40 per cent had been small farmers. Most of the mothers were educated too, 22 per cent of them having had a college education; they did, however, have a much higher rate of illiteracy than the men (30 per cent as against 15 per cent). I could mention here that, in general, the immigrants who have settled in Nottingham are a more educated group than our Birmingham sample. All families spoke exclusively Punjabi at home and indeed the whole ethos of the home was typically Punjabi in almost every aspect apart from the unexpectedly large percentage of mothers who go out to work (30 per cent).

Table 4.1: Findings of semi-structured interview

a) *Items showing change in attitude or practice*

1. Sleeping	:	79% sleep separately from mother.
2. Feeding	:	100% bottle-fed.
3. Grandparents	:	75% had no help from grandmother.
4. Toys	:	69% had soft-toys and/or small items.
5. Father participation	:	32% take baby for a walk.

b) *Items showing little change in attitude or practice*

Family	:	89% lived in extended family.
Mother substitute	:	80% child looked-after for part of the day.
Feeding	:	68% completely demand fed.
Physical punishment	:	100% horrified at the thought of smacking.
Sleeping	:	74% had no fixed hours.
Toilet Training	:	65% had no deliberate plan.
Independence	:	81% actively prevented independence.
Future planning	:	62% believed in long-term planning.
Educational toys	:	91% had none.
Educational training	:	nil — *i.e.* no mothers deliberately taught the child.

The findings of the semi-structured interview are tabulated above. The most striking change is that not one child was breast-fed. On further investigation it was found that the bottle was given to the baby by anyone who was available. It is possible that this lack of prolonged close contact with the mother might affect the healthy emotional development for which Indian children have hitherto been noted (Haynes, 1971). This breaking down of a rather intense emotional relationship is further affected by the radical change in sleeping-habits; invariably in India babies sleep with their mother giving them an absolute feeling of security. Furthermore, there is another gap in the emotional safety-net — the absence of grandparents in the family home, with whom, as I mentioned before, there is usually a very special relationship. Already some teachers have mentioned to me the differences in emotional stability between the Indian and British-born children. It is quite possible that the drastic changes in sleeping and feeding patterns, further exacerbated by the increasing trend for mothers to go out to work as soon as the children can go to a nursery, may lead to the undermining of the traditionally stability of the Punjabi child and family.

On many items where a change would help the child to cope with the British educational situation, parents still display the same attitudes as they would have had in Punjab. They buy few toys for the children, and practically no manipulative ones such as blocks, jigsaws, constructional toys, and they never deliberately teach them, *e.g.* point out aspects of the environment, teaching numbers and letters, purposive talking, reading stories. In fact, the parents were surprised that I should ask questions about attempting to teach children of this young age. Children are encouraged to play with other children rather than with things, and of course, this has a very positive aspect in that it fosters sociability and enables children to make and develop good relationships with other children.

The effect of this lack of educational training is exacerbated when school starts, by the absence of English in the home. As a matter of fact, these children are growing up in Punjabi houses in English cities and are not at all bilingual, though it was widely expected that they would be. The recent report by McEwen *et al.* (1975) found that even nursery schools do not make up this deficiency. It must be pointed out that this lack of educational training at home is not at all analogous to the English lower working class attitude of not valuing education. The very opposite is true. Indian families value education most highly, especially higher education, but they feel that it is the province of the teacher and the school and not the home. Another point in which there is a major difference between Punjabi and English families, and indeed schools, is in the amount of personal independence which the child is encouraged to develop. Most of the Punjabi mothers still cling to their children a great deal, and independent action is actively discouraged, particularly among girls. This cramping of the individuality is particularly seen in the paucity of Punjabi children's creative work when they go to school. It is worth noting that a few families are changing their attitude in this respect. At the same time, children may be helped somewhat in adjusting to new situations such as school by the fact that in most cases a mother substitute is employed to look after the baby for part of the day.

It is interesting to note the one item on which there has, perhaps thankfully, been no change at all in the traditional attitude — that of smacking pre-school children. Not only do Punjabi mothers not smack such children, but they were extremely horrified by the very idea of doing so. And an item which has a seemingly insignificant percentage, the extent of father participation in the child-rearing, is in fact very significant in the Punjabi sub-culture where there has hitherto never been the slightest participation by the father in the day-to-day upbringing of children. Actually, fathers take an active part only in planning the future of the child, especially the boys, and this long-term planning still seems to be a strong feature of the Punjabi community in matters of education, career and marriage.

Still very permissive in physical aspects like sleeping, eating, toilet training and discipline — all things which it is difficult and unnatural for a young child to regulate to a schedule, they have, however, adopted many English customs which they perhaps think make life easier, such as bottle-feeding and tins of baby food which are extensively used, either alone (25 per cent) or as part of a mixed Indian/English diet (63 per cent); and separate sleeping for the baby. Mother-substitutes are still relied on for part of the day, despite the absence of grandparents, but these are now sometimes friends or lodgers rather than close family. There is still a lack of awareness of the importance of perceptual skills, or pre-school experience and of the contribution that mothers can make to the developing mind.

Finally, there is a need for some organized teaching of English in playgroups and nursery schools, which at present tend to serve a neighbourhood whence come many children speaking Punjabi. This continues to be their language for most purposes, as they talk to each other and not to native children. This pattern is likely to continue in the absence of organized teaching of English.

Discussion of the Results

Cross-cultural research in the field of intellectual development provides an opportunity to test the universal validity of the theories and models developed in a particular context, and also to assess the importance of social and cultural factors on thinking processes. This research was designed to elucidate a number of important questions, two of these being fundamental ones:

1. The effects of a Western-type environment on the thinking processes and scholastic achievement of boys from the traditional culture of Punjab who have had full schooling in England.
2. The nature of thinking processes of indigenous Punjabi boys and their possible relationships to the social-cultural and educational background of the boys.

The reader will recall that a battery of tests was given to 140 boys. This sample came from three cultural groups, each of which was comprised of two age groups (9 to 9+, 11+). Thus six distinct groups were identified as follows:

English 9—9+	:	Referred to as E_J in the text
English 11+	:	Referred to as E_S in the text
British Punjabi 9—9+	:	Referred to as BP_J in the text
British Punjabi 11+	:	Referred to as BP_S in the text
Indigenous Punjabi 9—9+	:	Referred to as P_J in the text
Indigenous Punjabi 11+	:	Referred to as P_S in the text
'British groups'	:	Referred to as the four samples taken from Birmingham (UK) schools

All the boys were tested on coloured Raven Matrices, WISC Block Design, Conservation of Area and Weight and Vygotsky Blocks to assess their ability to form concepts. In addition, British groups were tested

Table 5.1: Means and standard deviations of groups on four tests

	WISC Blocks		Raven Matrices		Vygotsky Blocks		Draw-a-Man Test	
	M	SD	M	SD	M*	SD	M	SD
EJ	10.880	2.619	28.680	5.367	91.200	28.624	91.440	14.829
ES	9.520	2.931	28.400	6.076	82.000	27.763	90.200	15.489
EJ+S	10.200	2.835	28.540	5.675	86.600	28.292	90.820	15.020
BPJ	10.840	3.050	26.280	6.496	95.400	34.123	95.920	13.874
BPS	10.480	2.551	27.680	6.388	83.800	28.660	102.160	13.496
BPJ+S	10.660	2.789	26.980	6.415	89.600	31.733	99.04	13.907
PJ	4.550	3.561	12.000	4.230	119.750	27.790	—	—
PS	5.750	2.425	15.700	4.130	116.000	24.952	—	—
PJ+S	5.150	3.068	13.850	4.532	117.875	26.137	—	—

* = High scores imply low performance

Table 5.2: Result of conservation test

	Weight		Area		Volume	
	Successful	Unsuccessful	Successful	Unsuccessful	Successful	Unsuccessful
E_J	14	11	15	10	12	13
E_S	16	9	15	10	12	13
E_{J+S}	30	20	30	20	24	26
BP_J	16	9	11	14	10	15
BP_S	18	7	16	9	11	14
BP_{J+S}	34	16	27	23	21	29
P_J	7	13	2	18	–	–
P_S	15	5	7	13	–	–
P_{J+S}	22	18	9	31	–	–

on Conservation of Volume and Draw-a-Man tests. The means and standard deviations of the scores is presented in Table 5.1; and Table 5.2 shows the number of successful/unsuccessful boys on the conservation tests.

Firstly, it had to be established whether the performance of the British Punjabi groups is similar to the performance of the English groups and is different from that of the indigenous Punjabi groups. This was done by the use of 'Multi-variate Analysis of Variance', and the details of the results are shown in Table A.3 in Appendix A. Briefly, the inference drawn from the results is that the British Punjabi groups do not differ significantly* at .05 level from the English groups, but are significantly different from the two Punjabi groups. Subsequent analysis had to be done to find out the relative importance of each test to explain this differential performance. The statistical technique which was used on the data is referred to as 'discriminant analysis'**; its

* The difference between the groups is not due to chance: if the research is repeated with similar groups 100 times, difference of this nature would probably appear 95 times [19 out of 20]. In educational research generally, the minimum level of significance is taken to be at 5 per cent level. In this text if level of significance is not mentioned, it should be taken as 5 per cent level.

** Discriminant analyses was followed by analysis of variance and chi-square tests on quantitative and qualitative variables respectively. Furthermore, analysis of variance was followed by Schéffe test. For details see Ghuman, 1974.

function is to construct a linear combination of the given tests that will separate the groups maximally. The technical details of this analysis and its application to the data are to be found in the original work (Ghuman, 1974). Briefly, the relative importance of the tests which discriminate between the two indigenous Punjabi groups and the four British groups is as follows: Raven Matrices, WISC Blocks, Weight, Area and Vygotsky Blocks. The importance of this finding will be discussed later in this chapter.

It is now appropriate to discuss the performance of the boys in some detail and to seek possible explanations of their performance.

Raven Matrices Test

This test is designed to assess a person's clarity of observation and level of intellectual development. The data from the test can also reveal how far a person is able to reason by analogy. However, it is not claimed here that this test is culture-free and valid for all children, irrespective of their backgrounds and previous experiences; it was used in this research to investigate the influence of Western education on boys who belong to a traditional culture. Furthermore, it was hoped that the analyses of the Punjabi boys' responses would show up possible cognitive deficiencies within this group.

The Punjabi junior boys found the test interesting, but difficult (Mean = 12.0, SD = 4.23): five boys (25 per cent) of this group scored less than ten; their scores mainly consisted of correct responses given to the first eight items of set A and/or first three items of set Ab. According to the test manual such performances indicate 'that these children are only capable of answering items which are either composed of simple continuous pattern completion or discrete pattern completion, and are unable to respond correctly to items requiring completion of a pattern showing progressive changes and other designs involving the apprehension of the three figure as a related 'whole' to be completed by the fourth part (Raven, 1963, p. 32). The high scores (16+) attempted successfully most of the items from set A, approximately the first half of items from set Ab and the first three or four items from set B. None of the boys responded correctly to the second half of set Ab. For example, the typical answer to Ab9 was either 1, 3 or 5. Response number (1) shows the whole pattern when completed and (3) and (5) are repetitions of the parts of the given pattern. Thus we find that even the best in this group cannot analyse the perceived pattern into its constituent elements and distinguish between what is given and what he himself has to contribute.

The senior Punjabi boys are significantly better than the junior (Mean = 15.7, SD = 4.13), and show some progress, though their performance falls far short of even the junior Punjabi boys in this country, none scoring less than 10 and eight boys scoring more than 15 marks. However, even the best performers found it difficult to analyse the more complex Ab designs into their component parts and failed to respond correctly on such items. Furthermore, no boys were successful on other than the first three items of set B: instead of choosing the necessary correlative figures to complete the matrices, they chose one or other of the figures already given in the designs. The other common mistakes of the senior Punjabi boys, including the more successful ones, were those of orientation, i.e. they failed to choose figures with correct orientations to complete the matrices.

This test was also given, for the sake of interest, to a small group of non school-going illiterate boys of age range eight to ten years (No = 7, Mean = 8), whose performance was similar to those of the low scoring junior boys. The similarity of performance of school-going and non-school-going boys, from the same village, suggests that schools have failed to provide relevant experiences to these boys to overcome their basic perceptual difficulties. However, this conclusion is to be treated with caution as the numbers involved are very small.

We may conclude, then, that these boys find it difficult to work with this type of material, which is of a perceptual kind, and consequently cannot argue by analogy in this test. This I think is mainly due to their lack of experience and training, both at home and school with such materials as pictures, jigsaws and blocks. The degree of association found between this test and the cultural factor is high (.545), suggesting that the ability to perform well in it is indeed related to both the home and school environment. As could be expected, the Punjabi boys in England did significantly better on the Raven Matrices than the indigenous sample but they were not significantly different from the English sample. Similarly, when Ashby (1970) and Sharma (1971) compared the performances of Scottish and English children respectively, with that of long-stay immigrant children, they found no significant differences between them.

The surprising finding, however, is that the senior boys of the British Punjabi and English groups are not significantly better than the junior boys. The argument that the older boys might have come close to the maximum mark of 36 is not tenable, as the mean scores of the two older groups is well below the maximum mark (BP_S = 27.68, E_S = 28.40, BP_J = 26.28, E_J = 28.68). To clarify this position further, two groups each of 25 Welsh rural boys of similar social class background and age range were tested. The mean scores of these two groups (W_J = 27.36, SD = 5.58; W_S = 31.00, SD = 5.27) show that whilst the performance of this junior group is comparable to that of the junior boys in our samples, the senior Welsh boys were significantly superior to the Welsh junior boys to the British Punjabi senior boys and better, but not significantly so, than the English senior boys. These results suggest that the senior boys of the samples, on the whole, were doing less well than the boys of similar background in Wales. Hence, we may conclude that the low performance of the senior boys is not related to the ceiling limit of the test.

This tailing off of performance by the older boys of the Birmingham sample needs explanation. This may lie in the 'low expectation syndrome'. These schools have had very few successes at 11+ examinations in recent years. As a result it is quite likely that the class teachers did not expect many of their pupils to pass the examination and adjusted their teaching accordingly, whereas in the Welsh schools, successes at 11+ examination were considered to be a matter of great prestige and honour. During our visit to the rural schools in Wales, we found teachers devoting a substantial amount of time and energy in giving detailed practice and coaching in tests of intelligence and allied conceptual skills. These teachers expect a reasonably high performance from their pupils and stretch them accordingly. No doubt, this is also true of pupils in the middle class neighbourhood schools in Birmingham. Thus it is not unreasonable to suggest that the development of these boys might have been affected by the 'low expectation syndrome' (Pidgeon, 1970).

The analysis of the responses of the British Punjabi groups shows that the majority of these boys did not successfully solve the last few (3 or so) problems from the set Ab. Also the majority of them found the last three items of set B beyond their comprehension. This is due to the fact that they did not choose the required correlative figures, but selected figures which were already given in the matrices. For instance, the most common wrong answers to problem Ab_{12} (see Appendix B) were 1 and 4. The other more common mistakes were of orientation: for example in answer to B6, the most common responses were 5, 1 and 4. Number 5 reflects the error of orientation, whilst the other two errors are due to repetition of the figures given in the designs. However, these errors are made far less frequently as compared with those made by the Punjabi boys. The English boys made similar types of errors.

WISC Block Design Test

The performance of the Punjabi boys on this test was very poor, with the senior boys only marginally better than the junior boys (P_J = 4.55, SD = 3.56; P_S = 5.75, SD = 2.42). Seven junior boys and one senior boy failed to do even pattern C of the test. The major difficulty of the Punjabi boys seemed to lie in grasping the relation between two-dimensional designs and three-dimensional blocks. Furthermore, even the best subjects in this sample made errors of orientation: for instance, design number 3 was rotated through $180°$. These boys had never handled cubes or other similar material in schools or at home and consequently had great difficulty in manipulating them. A number of the subjects when making a design insisted on looking at the vertical side of the pattern they were making, despite the instructions that they should look on the top surface. None of the boys were successful in completing design 4 or any of the subsequent designs. (It is interesting to note that when this test was given to the son of a village carpenter, who was not included in our sample, he showed a quick grasp of the problems and successfully completed designs up to 6).

McFie (1961) also observed the orientation difficulties of African students in this type of test, and suggests that they are due to the lack of relevant background experiences. He provided such experiences to his subjects and there was an improvement in their performance. Lloyd and Pidgeon (1961) have also shown that coaching children in this type of task improves their performance. Vernon (1969) similarly comments on the low spatial ability of his testees who had little relevant experience with the material. Witkin (1966) has argued that the WISC Block Design test provides an excellent measure of field-dependence, but as far as this sample is concerned, this test seems to be of little value in assessing this factor as it is very difficult to say whether the low-scores of our Punjabi samples are indicative of field-dependence or are due to lack of appropriate perceptual experiences which leads to a low spatial ability. We cannot but surmise how far the researchers (Dawson, 1967; Berry, 1965) who have used this type of material to assess the bipolar dimension of field-independence and field-dependence are correct in deriving conclusions regarding child-rearing practices and the like, without first investigating the background experiences of their samples (perceptual experiences, spatial training, etc.). However, the use of this test has pin-pointed the precise nature of the difficulties which these boys experience; the problem or orientation with a spatial design, and the inability to relate two dimensional and three dimensional information.

The scores of the British Punjabi boys are not significantly different from those of the English boys. No differences due to age were expected as the scores are standardized with respect to this variable. The association between the cultural factor and performance on this test is high (= .401), again suggesting the importance of the nature of environment as a determinant of performance. Our findings support those of Sharma (1971) who found that long-stay Indian immigrant boys did not differ significantly from the English boys. Haynes' (1971) result is different from those of Sharma and of the present study, as she did not control social class and the children were considerably younger and as a result they had fewer years of school experience.

The boys in our sample, both British Punjabi and English, do not perform as well as Welsh rural boys of similar age and socioeconomic background. The mean scores of the Welsh boys (W_J = 11.52, SD = 3.15; W_S = 12.28, SD = 3.15) indicate that, whilst the performance of the junior boys in our samples (E_J = 10.88, SD = 2.62; BP_J = 10.840, SD = 3.15) is only marginally lower, the senior Welsh boys are significantly superior (at .01 level) to the senior English and the senior British Punjabi boys. This result reinforces the result reported on the Raven Matrices test and also the conclusion we have drawn regarding the performance of the senior boys of our sample.

We also compared the 'speed' of working of the three cultural groups. The bonus marks earned by the Punjabi boys were nil; whereas the British Punjabi boys earned high marks as 'bonus' — which were close to those of the English boys. No significant difference was found on the speed factor between these latter two groups (Table A.4).

To conclude, the British Punjabi boys who have had full schooling in this country have, unlike the indigenous Punjabi boys, developed their spatial ability and have also learned to work at speed. This reflects the value of previous experience in manipulation of three dimensional material given by English schools. We may note that the home interview schedule described in Chapter 4 shows the contribution of the home in this area to be negligible.

Conservation of Weight

The results of this test are interesting as no significant differences were found between the Punjabi, the British Punjabi and the English groups. The senior Punjabi boys are the best performers (C = 75 per cent, NC = 25 per cent). It is important to discuss the results of this test in detail as they are different from the results of all the other tests.

The Punjabi boys come from families which are engaged in traditional farming, where boys usually help their fathers in looking after the cattle and doing other chores, such as measuring, storing and weighing farm produce for sale. Thus these boys have considerable experience in measuring and weighing things at their homes and farms. It is reasonable to suggest that this previous experience helped these subjects, especially the older ones, to develop a pragmatic model to deal with such types of problems. Needless to say, older boys perform better partly due to sheer maturational factors, but also, I think, largely due to the fact that they are generally given more responsibility in the tasks described earlier.

The research of Price-Williams *et al.* (1967) with pottery-making children in Mexico showed that his testees were better conservers of amount than the control group children. Vernon (1969) has also shown, with Indian and Eskimo boys, the importance of specific experiences on performance in spatial and perceptual tests. Goodnow

(1969) also stressing the importance of previous experiences, of specific types on performance, quotes the remarks of a Chinese boy, who was successful in the Conservation of Weight test, as evidence to support her contention that previous experiences possibly provide 'a pragmatic model that serves as a landmark, a reference point or mnemonic device for pinning down a relationship and holding it in mind' (p. 259). However, it is arguable whether the good performance of our Punjabi boys was due to overlearning or whether they had genuinely internalized the measuring and weighing actions to form schemata, which are related to overall structures and are transferable to other tests of conservation. This point has to be considered again at a later stage.

It is apposite now to look at the behaviour and responses of the boys in some detail. The Punjabi boys were initially very nervous as they were not used to answering questions about subject matter on which they had not been given previous instructions by persons in authority. They were assured that their teachers would not be told the results of the test and that I was primarily interested in their individual responses, right or wrong. Even after these reassurances most of the boys were rather puzzled with the questions and looked for guidance. It was considered important not to give any facial perceptual cues (smiling, frowning and the like) during the testing sessions as they would have construed these expressions as marks of approval or disapproval. It is also interesting to note that the boys tended to pay more attention to the experimenter and his colleague than the task in hand; considerable tact and skill was needed to draw their attention to the problem in hand and elicit unprejudiced responses.

Their responses reflect similar processes of thinking to those found with the Western European children on conservation tests. Thus in response to the question: 'If I place this flat piece (a small chappati) on the scales, is it going to weigh the same, more or less than the ball?' Some typical successful responses would be as given below:

1. 'The same as the ball (pointing) as you have weighed them before.
2. 'The same as the ball as you have rolled the ball, having the same weight as this ball (pointing) into this shape'.

Typical wrong responses included:

1. 'Ball weighs more as it is round and the other one is flat'.
2. 'Ball weighs more — this is round and big (pointing) and this is flat'.
3. 'This (*pointing to flat piece*) weighs more'.

The successful answers were based on 'identity' (same-as-before type) rather than on reversibility (roll back into a ball — will weigh the same) or compensation (co-ordination of two dimensions). Thus our results confirm the stance taken by Bruner (1967C, p. 185) who states:

'. . . our argument is in sharp contrast to Piaget's. On purely logical grounds, we believe he has missed the heart of conservation. Both inversion and compensation to be effective must rest upon an appreciation of the original equality of quantities involved'.

He further argues (1967C, p. 201):

'. . . Reversibility and compensation could not by themselves be producing conservation — they are often encountered in instances in which the child has not achieved conservation'.

This debate between the Genevan and the Harvard school springs mainly from their different viewpoints; Piaget's model is embedded in logic and genetics, whereas Bruner's theoretical system is firmly rooted in psychological discourse. Consequently the results are interpreted through the respective conceptual frameworks.

The scores of the British Punjabi junior and senior boys are comparable to those of the English boys of their respective age groups, and furthermore the responses of the British Punjabi boys and the English boys are also very similar. Here are some of the typical successful answers:

1. 'Same weight — you flattened it and it increased only in size (pointing to the width), but stays the same weight'.
2. 'Same weight — you have only changed the shape'.
3. 'Same weight — you have neither added nor taken away any clay'.

These are, in substance, similar responses to those of the Punjabi boys. The typical responses of the unsuccessful boys were as follows:

1. 'This (flat piece) weighs less because you have squeezed it'.
2. 'This is broader — it must weigh more'.
3. 'Ball weighs more — because it is stronger'.

These boys, like the non-conserver Punjabi boys, were more concerned with the shape of the pieces, and seemed to infer that the weights of the ball and the flat piece depended on their respective shapes. In some ways this problem reminds us of the question which our own teachers in India used to ask: 'Which is heavier, a mound (Indian measure) of iron or cotton?' On the whole, the British Punjabi boys were far more articulate in giving their reasons for conservation as compared with the Punjabi boys, who often used the ostensive method of communicating their thinking and had to be questioned further.

The study of Vinh-Bang and Inhelder, briefly reported by Fogelman (1971) found that all the 11-year-old boys conserved weight and in the ten-year age group only 16 per cent failed to conserve. Compared with this sample, boys of our samples are considerably poorer in their performance.

Conservation of Area

Here the performance of the Punjabi boys was poorer than their performance on the conservation of weight test. There were only two conservers (10 per cent) in the junior group; the number conserving in the senior group was higher (35 per cent), but not significantly different from the junior group.

Our result is similar in some ways to one of the studies of Price-Williams and his colleagues (1967). In this study they found that potters' children, who had considerable experience with shaping and moulding materials, performed significantly better on conservation of amount, but not on conservation of weight and volume tests as compared with the control group children. Inhelder (1971) reported the results of a study with Algerian children, in which they were found to be relatively more successful on the conservation of amount than of length. The explanation offered is related to their previous experiences in measuring and storing quantities at home, which is analogous to our Punjabi sample. Inhelder (1971) argues that:

'... these children lack the kind of stimulation which results in more developed perceptual strategies ... they are not, as our Genevan children, made aware at a very early age of differences in height nor are they taught to compare length' (p. 163).

The Punjabi boys of our sample, whilst having considerable experience in weighing things, do not have experiences in measuring and assessing lengths and areas. Cultivation is on traditional lines and farmers do not bother to measure or assess before cultivation. The boundaries of the fields are fixed and seldom change, consequently there is little need to measure areas. However, the other possible explanation is that the test of Conservation of Area is more difficult than the Conservation of Weight test. In this test children are expected to do 'mental arithmetic': that four houses of the same size occupy the same area, no matter how they are arranged in the field, and this kind of thinking requires a greater degree of detachment from the personal field. Goodnow (1969) in her survey of cross-cultural researches concludes that children from less developed social milieux find it difficult to solve those cognitive problems which require some form of mental shuffling or transformation. Our results tend to support this contention.

Lastly, it is quite probably that the Punjabi boys were being influenced more by the practical rather than the logical considerations of the problem. From their everyday experience they might have formed the opinion that the 'spread-out houses' occupy more room as each of them needs a separate compound for the families, unlike the 'terraced houses' which usually have a communal compound. This was, to some extent, revealed by questions such as these: 'How much is the area to play?' 'Are they (animals) allowed to go near the doors and walls?'

The analysis of the responses of the Punjabi boys shows that the non-conservers were mislead by perceptual cues: 'Buffalo has more (*pointing*) — houses are in close together — these houses (*pointing*) are spread out'. All the non-conservers were asked: 'If I remove these houses — would the two animals have the same amount of grass?' Invariably the reply was 'yes'. The typical responses of the successful boys were as follows:

1. 'Both have the same, these are close — together (pointing): these are spread out (pointing); bu they occupy the same area'.
2. 'Both have the same, as the same number of houses are built on both sides'.

The performance of the British Punjabi boys is not significantly different from that of the English boys. Again, the surprising finding is that the older boys of these two combined cultural groups are not significantly superior to the younger boys.

The success of the British boys, both Punjabi and English, on this test is only marginally lower than on the Conservation of Weight test. In fact 46 per cent conserved on both the tests and 24 per cent did not conserve on either of the tests; 18 per cent conserved on weight but not in area and 12 per cent conserved in area but not in weight. The differing numbers of conservers on weight but not in area and vice versa can be interpreted as a chance result (X_2 = 1.2 with DF, NS at .05 level). Consequently such boys, unlike those reported in the previous cultural researches (including our Punjabi boys), have developed schemata to organize their perceptual experience, and are not solely relying on pragmatic models.

The typical responses of the British Punjabi conservers were:

1. 'They both have the same – all houses are the same size and take the same space'.
2. 'Same areas, as cow's houses don't make any difference, four houses just the same'.
3. 'Same amount to eat – take the same amount of room, because houses are the same size – they have got as much to eat as one another'.
4. 'They have the same (pointing to the houses) – they take the same amount of room – ones are spread out others are not'.

From the recorded responses of these boys and our personal impressions, we found that they were more articulate than the boys in Punjab, who often resorted to the ostensive method of explaining.

The unsuccessful British Punjabi boys gave the following type of responses:

1. 'No; he has got more to eat (*pointing to cow*). They are spread out and these are cramped together'.
2. 'Horse has less – cow's houses take only one part – horse's houses take more space'.
3. 'Different; horse has less and cow has more – four houses are in row – take less room than these (*pointing to spread out houses*)'.

Once again, we found the responses of these British Punjabi boys similar to the responses of the English and indeed the Punjabi boys. Hyde (1959) also concluded from her research in Aden that the responses of non-European children were similar to those of the children of European extraction, save that the former were poorer on all the Piagetian tests.

Hence, from these two tests of conservation we find evidence to substantiate the universal application of Piaget's model, at least as far as the concrete operational stage is concerned.

Conservation of Volume I

This test was given only to the British samples. The British Punjabi group is not significantly different from the English groups. Furthermore, senior boys are not significantly different from the junior boys. The number conserving on this test is slightly lower than on the other Piagetian tests of conservation used in this research; this is in line with the often found sequential progress in Conservation tests: Amount – Weight – Volume.

Further analysis was carried out on the conservation tests. It was considered interesting to work out the number of boys who conserved on all the tests, or any two of them, one of them, and none of them. It was hoped that such statistics would indicate the number of boys who had acquired/not acquired, as the case may be, the concrete stage of thinking. (Success in any two of the tests was considered adequate to show the acquisition of the concrete stage). The numbers conserving on all the tests in the samples are rather low, save the junior English boys who have a high success rate (44 per cent). The proportions conserving on two of the tests suggest that the senior boys are marginally better than the junior boys (Table A.5 in Appendix A). The total number of boys who have achieved the concrete stage of thinking, according to our criterion, in the composite British Punjabi sample is 31 (62 per cent), the corresponding figure for the composite English sample is 28 (56 per cent). There are 12 boys (24 per cent) in the British Punjabi sample and 11 boys (22 per cent) in the English group who did not conserve on any of the tests.

Conservation of Volume II

The success rate on this test was very low. There were only two (four per cent) conservers in the composite British Punjabi sample and four (eight per cent) conservers in the English composite sample. Typical incorrect responses were as follows:

'It (the lead ball) would push more water up as it's heavier than the plasticine ball'.

Similarly, in response to the question on 'ping pong ball' the answer was:

'It would push less water up — as it is lighter than the plasticine ball'.

Such poor responses may be due to the fact that they have not done any work of this type in school, and consequently fall back to the explanation which is perceptually more appealing, i.e. volume is related to weight of the subject.

Thus we may conclude that boys in our samples seem to explain volume of objects (in displacement experiments) by invoking their respective weights rather than size. Perhaps, without actual experience with this type of work, children find it difficult to relate volume with size. This result is not inconsistent with the results of the first experiment, in which one of the balls of clay was rolled into a sausage, i.e. the weight of the ball remained the same. Hence we found relatively more boys giving correct answers.

Goodenough-Harris Draw-a-Man Test

The results of this test shows that the British Punjabi composite group is significantly superior (at 0.01 level) to the English composite group. This is the only test on which significant difference was found between the composite cultural groups. On further analysis of the results, it became clear that, though the junior British Punjabi boys are better (but not significantly) than the junior English boys, the real differences are between the senior boys of the two cultural groups, British Punjabi boys being superior to the English boys. Our results do not support the findings of Ashby *et al.* (1970), who found even the long-stay immigrant children performing less well than the Scottish children. However, in their study the difference did not reach the significant level of .05. Haynes' (1971) Punjabi sample was significantly inferior to the English sample on a battery of tests, but not so on the Draw-a-Man test.

The reasons for this difference are difficult to explain save that the English boys on the whole did not do too well on the items involving 'sketching' and 'modelling' techniques. Whereas the British Punjabi boys, especially the seniors, earned quite a high mark on these items. It may be that English boys do not practise these skills even as frequently as do the Punjabi boys at home and at school, and consequently do less well on this test. However, what has emerged from the results is that the Punjabi immigrant boys perform reasonably well on the test which requires the ability to draw, and sketch, and which assumes a well-developed knowledge of the 'body-concept'.

Equivalence Test

The analysis of the responses and behaviour patterns of the Punjabi boys suggests that they were well motivated and enjoyed doing the test. They were rather pleased to see the pictures of objects, which were drawn pleasantly. The reason for this is not difficult to locate; there are few pictures of things in their books and there are no magazines and children's comics for them to read: furthermore, the few pictures they have in their books are in black and white. Almost all the boys recognized the things represented, but help was given whenever the boys failed to identify the objects in question.

We briefly mentioned in Chapter Three the conceptual framework used to analyse the sorting behaviour of the subjects. It is appropriate now to discuss in some detail the attibutes used by the subjects in making their groups and the structure of these groupings.

The following categories were used to classify the attributes:

1. Perceptible:
    a) Colour: water pump and aeroplane: 'They are both blue'.
    b) Shape: apple and clock: 'They are a round shape'.
    c) Spatial: doll, scissors, coat and house: 'They all go in this house' (pointing to the first three).

2. Functional:
   a) Hammer, saw, nails: 'You can mend things with them'.
   b) Apple and pumpkin: 'Apple to eat and pumpkin to eat'.

3. Nominal:
   A conventional linguistic name is used to group the objects:
   a) Hammer, saw and scissors: 'These are tools'.
   b) Car, bus, aeroplane: 'They are transport'.

Other types of attributes
   1. Affective:
      Aeroplane and doll: 'I like to play with them'.
   2. Rhymes:
      'Parrot and carrot'.
      'Brolly and dolly'.
   3. Fiat:
      When no reason is given for grouping, even after prompting (none
      of the boys responded in this fashion).

The structure of the groupings was classified into three major types,
following the scheme developed by Olver and Hornsby (1966). These
are given below:

1. Superordinate groupings:
   a) General superordinates: when grouping is constructed on the
      basis of attributes which are common to all the objects in the
      group, e.g. saw, hammer, scissors: 'These are all tools'.
   b) Itemized superordinate: In this type of grouping, the objects are
      united together with a common feature, the basis on which each
      object is added to the group is clearly stated. For example: lamp,
      candle and sun: 'This gives light (*pointing to lamp*) and so does
      the candle and sun shines and gives light'.

2. Complexive groupings:
   In these types of groupings a subject forms a group by selecting a
   number of attributes none of which is common to all the objects.
   Following Vygotsky's 1962 research, Olver and Hornsby (1966)
   and Davey (1968) used four sub-types; but the responses of the
   boys in this research could largely be described by the following
   two:

   a) Collection complex: the subject mentions different attributes for
      each object, feature, e.g. radio and cycle:
         'Cycle is to ride and radio tells time and news'.

b) Chain complexes: These are formed when the subject groups objects which are related to the object proceeding it, e.g. water-pump, tree and parrot: 'Water-pump gives water to the tree and parrot sits on the tree'.

3. Thematic groupings:

The objects are related together by some theme, which is imagined by the subject, e.g. doll, coin and aeroplane:

'Doll needs money to go on the aeroplane'.

This mode was often used by the boys to group two things together, e.g. 'dogs chase rabbits'. In these instances it was not always possible to assess accurately the attributes used in forming groups; hence in our classification of attributes, 'no attribute' category refers to groupings based on this mode.

Attributes used for Groupings

In table 5.3 are presented the attributes used by the various samples forming their groupings. The reader will recall that each boy was asked to make ten attempts at the sorting task; however, a number of boys did not make the maximum number of attempts.

The statistical analysis (X^2 Chi-square) showed that the four British groups were significantly different at .001 level, from the two Punjabi groups.

Examination of the responses shows that colour has been used predominantly by the Punjabi boys, whereas the boys from the other samples hardly used this attribute for grouping. However, we may note here that the Punjabi senior boys use this attribute less often than the Punjabi junior boys. All the British samples prefer to form their groupings either on function or by using an existing linguistic category, i.e. common name. But the Punjabi boys, especially the junior ones, use these attributes far less frequently to form their groupings. Again, we find the Punjabi senior group to be better than the junior in the use of nominal and functional categories. Both the English and the British Punjabi senior boys are significantly different from their respective junior fellows. Whilst the difference between the English samples is primarily due to the excessive use of the thematic style of responding (NA) by the senior group; the difference between the British Punjabi samples lies in the fact that the junior boys tend to use more thematic and fewer nominal attributes. This descrepant result between the two cultural groups is hard to explain.

We have graphed (No. 1) the perceptible (colour, shape) and non-perceptible (functional and nominal) attributes of the six groups to compare and contrast their performance. It is clear from this graph that

Table 5.3: The types of attributes used by the six groups in the Equivalence Test

Group	Colour	Shape	Function	Nominal	N/A	Rhyme	Affective	Total	Maximum Possible
EJ	1	1	104	60	14	2	2	184	25 x 10 = 250
ES	—	4	108	54	37	3	—	206	250
EJ+S	1	5	212	114	51	5	2	390	500
BPJ	6	7	92	46	33	5	5	194	250
BPS	2	2	97	66	16	4	—	187	250
BPJ+S	8	9	189	112	49	9	5	381	500
PJ	71	—	18	9	27	—	3	128	20 x 10 = 200
P S	55	—	50	15	21	3	—	144	200
PJ+S	126	—	68	24	48	3	3	272	400

Table 5.4: Strategies used by the six groups in the Equivalence Test

	Superordinate	Itemized Superordinate	Collection	Chaining	Thematic	Total	Maximum Possible
Ej	146	9	5	4	20	184	250
Es	136	14	5	3	48	206	250
Ej+s	282	23	10	7	68	390	500
BPj	127	10	16	4	37	194	250
BPs	162	4	3	3	15	187	250
BPj+s	289	14	19	7	52	381	500
Pj	54	6	37	4	27	128	200
Ps	82	15	26	5	16	144	200
Pj+s	136	21	63	9	43	272	400

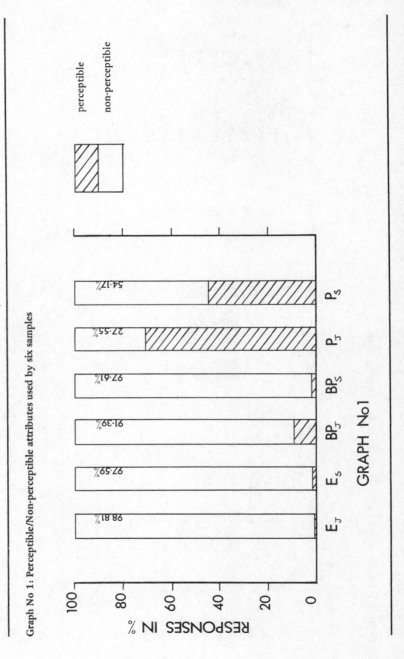

Graph No 1: Perceptible/Non-perceptible attributes used by six samples

the dominant mode of grouping used by the Punjabi junior boys is perceptible. They tend to rely on surface qualities of the objects to form equivalence, whereas the senior boys show progress and look for the functional relationship between/among objects or existing lexicons in the language. All the British boys seem to rely on non-perceptible attributes with few exceptions. This finding is in agreement with the researches of Evans and Segall (1969), Serpelo (1969) and Maccoby and Modiano (1969). There is quite a high proportion of thematic responses in all the samples, and because of this we find a rather high proportion of responses in the no-attribute category. The other types of attributes, e.g. affective rhyme are too infrequently used to merit interpretation.

The preference for perceptual groupings of the Punjabi boys can be explained if we examine the nature of the environment in which they are being brought up. They live in small villages with fewer artefacts to understand and are exposed to less complex environments as compared with the urban children. In this type of environment, they learn to identify things by acute perceptual observation. Streets and houses have no names and numbers, and have to be located by reference to colour, size or spatial proximity to a conspicuous object (a tree, a well, a pond, etc). It is an interesting experience to ask a child or an adult the whereabouts of a person in a village. Inevitably the answer would be something like this: 'He lives in a big red house near the well'. On the farms, these boys are told to look for perceptual differences when examining the type of grasses and crops. Schools, with their emphasis on rote learning, do not provide sufficient experiences in sorting and the like, and consequently these children learn to look for 'surface' differences. The use of names to label objects is similarly less often used in everyday life. The ostensive method, e.g. pointing, showing, is preferred.

Structure of groupings

The results are presented in Table 5.4. Again by the use of the Chi-square test it was inferred that the English composite group is not significantly different from the British Punjabi composite group; but the British Punjabi and the English composite groups are significantly different from the Punjabi composite group. The examination of the responses shows that the Punjabi boys make complexive groupings (collection and chaining) more frequently than the British boys and the converse of this is true if we consider superordinate groupings. The differences on the thematic category among the composite groups are only marginal (P = 15.8 per cent, E = 17.4 per cent BP = 13.6 per cent). However, we must point out that even the Punjabi boys make superordinate groupings more frequently than complexive groupings (P_S = 57 per cent, P_J = 26 per cent) and that the association between the type of attribute used (colour) and the strategy used for groupings is not that high. In this respect our result does not agree with Olver and Hornsby (1966) who claimed to have found an association between the type of attributes used and the structure of grouping in younger children. However, our result is in agreement with Davey (1968) who found that boys using superordinate groupings tend to use the attribute of theme as frequently as they used non-perceptible attributes.

The analysis of the responses of the six individual groups shows interesting results. The Punjabi senior boys are better on superordinate groupings, but only marginally different from the junior boys on the complexive responses. Furthermore, they use thematic responses less frequently than the juniors. The British Punjabi senior group is significantly different from the junior group; there are a high proportion of superordinate and a low proportion of complexive and thematic groupings as compared with the juniors. From these two groups (BP and P) we may deduce that the younger boys use thematic groupings more often than the older boys, and the older boys tend to use superordinate grouping more frequently than the younger ones, again in agreement with the findings of Olver and Hornsby (1966) who found a decrease in thematic grouping with increasing age and an increase in superordinate groupings. However, the analysis of the English boys' responses is not in line with the above conclusion. Here, we find the younger group to be better on the superordinate grouping and the older to be better on thematic grouping; there is little difference on complexive grouping. This result is difficult to explain save that the younger group has performed marginally better on tests of Raven Matrices, WISC Block Design and may be showing a better performance on this test because of their all-round superior general cognitive abilities.

The boys in all the samples, except British Punjabi senior boys, showed preference for pairing. For example a boy would group, say, scissors and saw and call them tools on his first grouping, and would again pick up a hammer and a saw and refer to them as tools. Of course, it is likely that these boys would have formed groups with more than two objects, had they been asked to do so. But in this research the aim was to study the free-sorting behaviour of the boys; and no limitations were placed on their groupings. This is contrary to Olver and Hornsby (1966) who found only 25 per cent of the 11 year-old boys forming pairs in their grouping, but in line with Davey's (1968) research among Tristan da Cunhna children. He found the children of the junior age group (nine years nine months) and even of the senior age group (12 years) to prefer pairing.

Pairing may be interpreted as an extreme form of realism. The child notices similarities between two objects and unites them either with a perceptible attribute or uses a word to name them. He does not use this rule systematically to include more items in his group. From our impressionistic examination of the data, we found that the boys who preferred pairings also used perceptible, nominal and thematic modes to form their groupings, whereas the boys who grouped more than two items tended to use function as an attribute. Thus there is a fair degree of support for linking pairing with realism.

The average number of groups made by the subjects, in some ways, reflects the degree of flexibility and fluency in their thinking. From Table 5.5. we find the composite Punjabi group to be the lowest; and little difference existing between the British Punjabi and the English boys. A not unjustifiable conclusion to be drawn from this result is that the Punjabi boys are less flexible and fluent than the British boys.

Table 5.5: Average number of groups made by the six samples

	Average groups	*Maximum*
E_J	7.36	10
E_S	8.24	10
E_{J+S}	7.8	10
BP_J	7.76	10
BP_S	7.48	10
BP_{J+S}	7.62	10
P_j	6.4	10
P_S	7.2	10
P_{J+S}	6.8	10

Table 5.6: Number of subjects using the 'three major strategies' on the Vygotsky Block Test

	Syncretic	*Complexive**	*Conceptual*
P_J	16	20	0
P_S	12	20	1
BP_J	8	24	2
BP_S	6	24	5
E_J	7	25	5
E_S	6	24	4

* Complexive phase includes all the sub-phases, collection, chain complex, etc.

We may summarize from our results that the Punjabi boys who are being brought up in rural environments used different attributes and also structured their groupings differently from the boys who have the same ethnic origin, but live in an urban environment. The former tend to prefer colour as a grouping attribute whereas the British Punjabi boys prefer functional and nominal attributes. Furthermore, they use complexive structures more frequently than the British Punjabi boys, who employ superordinate structures. Thus, to conclude, we may state that the Punjabi boys, especially the younger ones, are perceptually orientated, less flexible and fluent, and are less abstract in forming groups based on equivalence.

Vygotsky Blocks

The analysis of the quantitative data on this test supports our major hypothesis that the British Punjabi group is significantly superior to the Punjabi group. We found no significant differences between the composite British Punjabi and the composite English samples. This test was found difficult by most of the boys in our samples. Inspection of Table 5.6 confirms this inference. There were no solutions of grade one in Punjabi groups; the British Punjabi and English groups had only 2 and 4 solutions respectively in this category.

The performance of the Punjabi junior boys was the poorest. Three boys did not even complete the test satisfactorily when all the blocks were upturned. However, even when we include these boys with others who did sort out the blocks correctly, but were not successful in resorting (grade 5 solution), the proportion giving a poor solution is still very high indeed (70 per cent); only six boys (30 per cent) re-sorted correctly (see table 5.7). Thus we may conclude that these boys were perceptually orientated and found it difficult to abstract attributes for correct grouping, even when cues were provided for doing so.

Table 5.7: Number of subjects attaining the various grades of solution on the Vygotsky Blocks Test

		Grade of Solution					
	Failure	*5*	*4*	*3*	*2*	*1*	*Total*
P_J	3	11	3	3	0	0	20
P_S	1	8	8	2	1	0	20
BP_J	–	8	4	9	3	1	25
BP_S	–	5	5	9	5	1	25
E_J	–	6	7	6	4	2	25
E_S	–	4	6	9	4	2	25

This result is in line with the equivalence test, in which we found a large proportion of the boys using colour as an attribute of grouping and employing complexive and thematic strategies for structuring their sorting procedures. The Punjabi senior boys performed relatively better on this test: only one of the boys did not complete the test, showing a distinct improvement on this test. Forty per cent of the boys, however, could not resort the blocks correctly, and there was only one boy whose solution fell in grade 2. Thus their performance shows a distinct improvement on this test: again in line with the results of the equivalence test. The performance of the British Punjabi boys was superior to that of the Punjabi boys. There were only five senior and eight junior boys who could not resort the blocks correctly. The modal location of the correct solution fell in grade 3, i.e. the one based on interrelationships of the groups, e.g. these are the largest — smallest, and so on.

The English group show a similar pattern of solution except that the junior boys produced fewer grade 3 solutions. We can deduce from this that the Punjabi groups needed far more cues than the other groups to do the correct sorting. The British Punjabi and the English junior boys needed slightly more cues than the senior boys of these respective groups.

We now consider the strategies employed by the various groups in the sortings. Three main phases were postulated and empirically validated by Vygotsky (1962). Stones and Heslop (1968) confirmed these findings with an English sample of high socioeconomic background.

The numbers of boys using the main strategies are given in Table 5.6. Inspection of the table leads us to conclude the dominant strategy used by the boys, irrespective of age and cultural affiliation is complexive (all the sub-types have been included in this category). The major difference between the Punjabi and British samples lies in their use of vague syncretic and conceptual strategies. We find only one senior boy from the Punjabis who showed true conceptual thinking as opposed to seven (five senior and two junior) from the British Punjabi and nine (five junior and four senior) from the English boys. The vague syncretic category is very largely composed of boys who resorted to 'trial and error' after unsuccessful attempts to sort by colour and shape or who got frustrated and consequently did random shifting of blocks. Thus we interpret it as a reaction to a stress situation rather than a conscious strategy adopted by the subjects.

The typical response of conceptual thinkers was to start sorting by shape, and when this was not successful, to try colour. After a few complexive sortings, they then tried size; finally, such conceptual thinkers then made use of the nonsensical words to abstract and synthesize the principle underlying the correct solution. On the other hand the boys who achieved grade 5 solutions, largely used only complexive strategies; but they also resorted to trial and error when they made many abortive attempts. They seemed to be carried away, as it were, by perceptual similarities of the blocks and were unable to keep the abstracted attribute intact.

Our results are substantially in agreement with Stones and Heslop (1968), in which they found all the ten-year-olds and 70 per cent of 11-year-olds making use of complexive strategies. However, the number of boys showing true conceptual thinking in their sample far exceeds the numbers in our samples. This difference, in our opinion, is the result of the low social class background of our samples.

Finally, we report the correlation between this test and Raven Matrices and WISC Block Design tests respectively. The correlation between this test and Raven Matrices in the British sample ($E_J + E_S + BP_J + BP_S$) was found to be $-.33^*$ (significant at .01 level), which is not high but close to the correlation reported by other research workers, e.g. Semenoff and Laird (1952). Similarly we found a correlation of $-.47$ (again significant at .01 level) with this test and WISC Block Design test. Thus we can conclude that this test partially samples the same abilities ('g' and 'k') as the other two tests, and at the same time provides information on the level of conceptual development of the subjects.

Our detailed analyses of the Punjabi boys' responses have elucidated the nature of their thinking processes, and also the difficulties that they faced in doing the tests, which are partly a reflection of the subjects' lack of experience of test taking situations. In our research we tried to minimize some of the problems which are usually faced by researchers engaged in cross-cultural work. The tests were given in the native language and familiar materials were used in the Piagetian tests and the test of equivalence. As I come from one of the villages from which the sample was drawn, and have an empathy with the social and cultural life of the community, it was easy to form a very good rapport with the boys. The informal atmosphere in which these tests were given further helped to secure good motivation.

We have already discussed the nature of the tests used and the constructs and theories on which they are based. Suffice it to say that the conservation problems and the equivalence test assess psychological behaviours which are ubiquitous; all communities in some ways have come to terms with conservation problems; e.g. objects and amounts,

---

* The correlation is negative because high scores on Vygotsky Blocks are indicative of poor performance and vice versa in case of WISC and RM.

and also have well established practices for classifying things and events. We may conclude, then, that in our research we were making genuine attempts to understand psychological processes employed by the boys in solving problems related to the basic fundamental cognitive activities of man.

However, our use of the Raven Matrices and WISC Block Design tests does not fall within the categories discussed above. We cannot be sure that the tests were measuring the same abilities (g and k) which they are designed to measure because these boys have little previous experience with the type of material used in these tests. It would seem that the most useful tests for assessing the intellectual abilities of the Punjabi boys are the ones which can be given informally and consist of materials known to the subjects. Piagetian tests and the test of equivalence (e.g. the one used in this study or of other authors) in this respect, seem to be the most suitable. The Vygotsky Blocks test is too difficult and as a consequence can lower the motivation of children of this ability range. However, time permitting, it is useful for pinpointing the concept-formation strategies of the children. The Raven Matrices and other such formally constructed tests can serve a useful diagnostic purpose, e.g. to pinpoint the cognitive area in which these subjects are not making progress when judged against the established norms.

In sum, then, we have found the British Punjabi boys to be remarkably similar to the English boys in their responses, both quantitatively and qualitatively; whereas significant differences in quality as well as quantity of thinking were found between the indigenous Punjabi and the British Punjabi groups. Both the junior and the senior Punjabi boys are poorer in their performance on all the tests except on the test of Conservation of Weight. Their performance on the Raven Matrices test showed that they were global in their perception and were unable to analyse the problems objectively. They could not analyse the perceived whole into its component parts and distinguish between what is given and what is required. These characteristics according to Bruner (1967a) reflect the iconic style of representation and are also to some extent an indication of field-dependence. Their other common error was of orientation; they were unable to locate a figure's orientation with respect to themselves and other objects in the field. This was confirmed in our analysis of the Block Design test. Their poor performance on this test is also an indication of poorly developed spatial-ability, which is an important predictor of technical-mechanical aptitude. However, from their poor performance we cannot conclude that they also lack the ability to 'induce' as they have had no experience with this type of material either at home or in school. Their responses on the Conservation of Area test showed their excessive reliance on perceptual rather than conceptual aspects of the problem.

They were unable to distinguish between the real and the apparent change and consequently made illogical judgements.

This heavy perceptual bias in the orientation of the boys is further reflected in their responses to the test of equivalence and Vygotsky Blocks. In forming equivalence groups, they predominantly used colour as an attribute of objects. The choice of functional and nominal categories, on the other hand, is an indication of the ability to go beyond the surface qualities of the objects and search for deeper relationships between/among objects. In other words, sorting by non-perceptible attributes involves the use of the higher mental processes (abstraction, generalization, etc.) which these boys did not use. In the concept-formation test a high proportion of the subjects could not re-sort the blocks correctly, despite the cues provided. This suggests that they were unable to abstract the relevant attributes from the blocks to form the concept, and their first successful sorting was based on perceptual rather than conceptual considerations. Thus we have found the Punjabi boys to be perceptually orientated, rigid in their thinking and operating at lower levels of abstraction.

The test data also provided us with the opportunity to comment on the type and nature of the language used by the boys. In the Equivalence test the use of existing names e.g. tools to group the objects, was minimal as compared with the attribute of colour. This is not due to lack of proper nouns in the Punjabi language, but rather shows a general preference for surface qualities of the objects. Furthermore, they tended to use labelling (red, brown) and pointing far more frequently than sentences to describe their groupings. In Piagetian tests, these boys used the most restricted form of the language in their explanations. They found it extremely difficult to articulate their reasons by the use of proper sentences and had to resort to pointing for their explanations. In other words, their use of the language was closely tied to the context. Similarly, their poor performance with Vygotsky Blocks is an indication of their inability to use words as an aid to thinking and concept formation. We may conclude, then, that these boys tend not to use language for cognitive planning, structuring and synthesising their sensory experiences. This cannot be attributed to the deficiency in the language (syntax, grammar, vocabulary, etc.) but to lack of training, both at school and at home, in relating language to practical experiences.

Explanation of performance

It is now appropriate to look for a possible explanation of their poor performance. The genetic explanation is not tenable as the Punjabi boys in this country who belong to the same ethnic group perform just as well as the indigenous English boys. So we focus our attention on socio-cultural and educational factors for possible explanations.

These boys live in rural environments which are simple. The social system is based on face-to-face interaaction, the network of relationships is limited and the communication is mostly direct. As a consequence, there are relatively fewer demands placed on them to use abstract styles of thinking. It would also be correct to say that physical identification of objects and persons is important for effective role playing in a close-knit traditional community. A child adopting a symbolic mode of interpretation of reality would be considerably handicapped in his social adjustment. In Bruner (1967, p. 27) Khulman argues that a conceptual child gains the ability to abstract and analyse, but loses his ability to preserve the distinctive quality of perceptual experiences as such. A major value-orientation of this community is collective as opposed to individualistic. The community nurtures a strong belief in corporate life; social conformity is prized and deviants are rigidly controlled through social sanctions. Elders, especially those in authority, are held in great respect, and their judgements, pronouncements and views on nature, society, religion and social events are sacrosant. These values are reflected in the child-rearing practices (see Chapter 4 p. 61). There is very little of what Bruner calls contingent dialogue between the child and the adults in the family. The children are treated as receptacles which are to be filled with the social and elementary technical know-how of the community. This type of training is not conducive, according to Witkin (1966), to analytical and independent thinking. Thus we found our boys to be subdued in their attitudes and concrete, global and synthetic in their cognitive style.

The technical know-how of this community is limited. There are very few scientific concepts used in everyday social exchanges and the possession of technological objects is confined to only a handful of people. Because of the rigid system of stratification (castes) and the division of labour, the members of this community do not engage in woodwork, metalwork, painting and designing activities which are considered to provide spatial and perceptual experiences. In summary, we can state that the amplifiers, to use Bruner's term, provided by the community for these boys are not adequate to push the cognitive development from the iconic to the symbolic mode of representation.

Lastly, we evaluate the impact of formal schooling on the intellectual development of these indigenous Punjabi boys. Formal schooling, according to Greenfield and Bruner (1966) can provide children with the opportunity to learn about the world in a non-action context, and such learning promotes good structuring of experiences. For example, the use of written language in schools forces the children to plan and structure their thoughts prior to writing, as the written communication has to be understood without concrete cues. Furthermore, there is a contingent dialogue between the teacher and the pupils which helps the children to see contradictions between 'what things look like and what they really are'. This stance is supported by the findings of an empirical study done with the Wolof school-going and illiterate children.

However, in our research the performance of the senior Punjabi boys, who have been in schools for at least three and a half years, falls far short of the performance of even the Junior British Punjabi boys. This leads us to conclude that the education which these children receive must be of a very poor quality in terms of the objectives of our inquiry. Our description of schools (see Chapter 4, p.   ) confirms our view. We found the teaching in these schools to be entirely mechanistic. Teachers are obliged to handle large classes and consequently use drill method for teaching the basic skills. The authority of the teachers is supreme in school; no child ever dares to question the views and interpretations given by the teachers. There is no opportunity for children to explore, manipulate and make things for themselves. As a consequence, schools fail to provide the necessary experiences and intellectual stimulation which are necessary for the development of higher mental processes. One wonders whether the intellectual development of these boys is in any way enhanced by this type of schooling. What emerges from our discussion on schooling is that researchers ought to describe the type of education imparted to children when the factor of schooling is mentioned, otherwise it 'is likely to lead to erroneous conclusions regarding the role of the school in intellectual development. As we have shown, what goes on in the schools is of crucial importance. To summarize, the boys in our sample are poor in their performance owing to lack of perceptual-kinesthetic experiences, poor use of the language, stultified curiosity and imagination, as well as rigid, inflexible attitudes which are acquired from their elders.

The findings of our research demonstrate possible short-comings of the education which is currently given to the Punjabi primary school children. If this is a universal state of affairs throughout India — there is no reason to believe this is not so, as Punjab is the most prosperous state — the future of India may be considered to be in question. There is a desperate demand for resourceful engineers, scientists and the like to develop the resources of the country. However, the educational experiences transmitted are hardly conducive to the development of conceptual and spatial abilities which are necessary for both scientific and technical know-how.

We now summarize the intellectual achievement of the British Punjabi boys in order to discern their cognitive style. These boys, on the whole, find little difficulty in objective analysis of the perceptual fields. They have well developed spatial and general ability as assessed by the WISC Block Design test. They can competently analyse two dimensional design forms, and are able to re-structure the same design forms when working three dimensionally; this ability was conspicuously absent in the indigenous Punjabi sample. Their responses on the Equivalence test show they prefer to form their groups on functional and nominal attributes, and use superordinate rules to structure their groupings. Equally, their performance also shows that they prefer to use sentences as opposed to labelling and pointing modes to explain their reasons for their groupings. As far as the Vygotsky test is concerned, it is evident that a high proportion of these boys are capable of forming concepts with the help of cues, but are not capable, as yet, (except for a few boys) of thinking at a true conceptual level. However, we must point out that this advanced level of thinking, involving the formulation and systematic evaluation of hypotheses, can only be expected of boys of high intellectual ability.

Their general achievement level on Piagetian tests shows that they are not led by surface qualities of the objects and are capable of looking for deeper relationships. The indications are, therefore, that in the majority of cases (62 per cent) the boys have acquired the ability to think with an internalized, reversible and co-ordinated action system which in Piaget's theory is designated as a stage of concrete operations. In their answers on these tests, they were far more articulate than the Punjabi boys; unlike the native Punjabi boys, they were lively, inquisitive and free in their conversation and uninhibited in demeanour. At times it was difficult to believe that the immigrants belonged to the same ethnic groups as the boys in the Punjab. Thus to summarize, the British Punjabi boys think at a more abstract and analytical level, have well developed spatial ability and tend to use language to structure and organize their experiences.

In conclusion, we may assert that the performance of the two British groups (BP$_{J+S}$ and E$_{J+S}$) is very similar. In this respect our study differs from that of Lesser *et al.* (1965) who draw other conclusions regarding the different patterns of abilities of subjects belonging to different ethnic groups.

In our discussion we have been concerned, so far, only with the evaluation of the basic thinking processes of the British Punjabi boys and have not examined their scholastic abilities and attitudes to school. The reader will recall (Chapter 3) that class teachers were asked to rate the abilities of the British Punjabi and the English boys on spoken English, understanding of English, written English and Arithmetic. The results are presented in Table 5.8 This statistical finding suggests that the English boys are rated significantly higher than the Punjabi boys on their spoken English, and comprehension of it. However, no such conclusion can be drawn regarding the abilities in written English and

Arithmetic, i.e. English and the British Punjabi boys get roughly similar ratings on these two abilities.

Table 5.8: Chi-square test on abilities and attitudes of BP$_{J+S}$ and E$_{J+S}$ groups

		X^2	DF	P
1.	Ability in Spoken English	15.49	3*	<.005
2.	Ability to write English	0.864	3*	NS
3.	Ability to understand English	12.04	3*	<.01
4.	Ability in Arithmetic	6.42	3*	NS
5.	Attitude to School and Learning	1.17	3*	NS
6.	Parents attitude to School and Education	3.54	3*	NS
7.	Participation in School activities	6.18	4	NS

* There were five categories in all [A, B, C, D and E], but because of the small numbers in categories D and E they were combined for analysis.

Our results lead us to conclude that no significant differences exist between the two cultural groups on predominantly school-based activities, but the British Punjabi boys are rated lower on those activities which also take place in the home environment. This is not surprising in view of the fact that little English is spoken in their homes, and that these families are still fully immersed in the Punjabi culture. According to the head teachers, boys spoke practically no English when they were admitted to infant schools; thus the present level of achievement in English is entirely due to the experience and training they have had at school. In contrast Ashby *et al.* (1970) found a long-stay immigrant group (nine years stay) to be marginally better, (but not significantly) on oral English, English reading and written English and Arithmetic than the Scottish children. The discrepant result may be due to the nature of the samples; our sample is entirely composed of Punjabi boys, whereas Ashby's included children from the whole of the sub-continent of India and Pakistan.

The attitudes to school and learning of the British Punjabi groups are not rated any more favourably than those of the English boys. In this respect our result differs from Haynes (1970) who found a significant difference (in favour of Punjabi children) between the Punjabi and the English group. This may be due to the differences in the type of instruments used for assessing this attitude. We used teachers' ratings, whereas Haynes employed a pupils' school questionnaire devised by Lunn (1970). Teachers do not rate these two groups differently on their participation in school activities such as school trips, drama and school teams. Similarly, no significant difference on rating on parents' attitude was found. Thus it can be concluded that these British Punjabi boys are as well disposed to schooling and its activities as their indigenous English classmates.

We have shown quite clearly that the British Punjabi boys who have had full schooling in this country are, on the whole, not different in their basic thinking processes, scholastic achievement and attitude orientations from the English boys. However, we wished to investigate further the crucial importance of Western-type education in the intellectual development of the British Punjabi boys. To achieve this end we had to assess the home background of these boys. Three dimensions were researched: use of language, adoption of English norms, and educational experience provided by the families. The information was collected by personal interviews of a semi-structured nature. The results of these interviews are presented in Tables 5.9 — 5.12. It is clear from Table 5.9 that almost all these boys speak Punjabi with their parents, and only six per cent speak in English with their brothers and sisters. However, the proportion of families which take an English newspaper is fairly high (36 per cent).

Let us consider their responses on items relating to the interaction with, and adoption of norms, of the host culture (Table 5.10). We find they still prefer to have fairly large families, preserve their own dietetic habits, rarely visit or are visited by English friends and none of them provides individual rooms for their children. The boys make friends with their own kind, listen to their own music and go to the Indian pictures for entertainment with their families. However, we find that a significantly higher proportion celebrate Christmas and childrens' birthdays and have adopted the English custom of giving pocket money to the children. Thus we see a slight conformity on those cultural patterns which are directly concerned with the children. From the results of Table 5.11 it may be inferred that they are almost fully immersed in their own religion, and quite a high proportion (38 per cent) of these parents also send their boys to learn Punjabi on Sundays in Sikh temples.

Table 5.9: Percentage responses of British Punjabi boys on items relating to the use of the English language

	Punjabi	English	Mixed	None
Language of parents	96	—	4	—
Language with parents	94	—	6	—
Language with siblings	48	6	46	—
Parents paper	14	36	12	38

Table 5.10: Percentage responses of British Punjabi boys on items relating to adoption of English norms

Nature of families:	Extended	48	Nuclear:	52
Size of families:	Small (3 or less)	16	Large (4 or more)	84
		No		Yes
Visits from English people		92		8 (including school teachers)
Visit English homes		94		6
Celebrate Christmas		17		83
Mother at work		66		34
Birthday celebration		26		74
Own room		100		—
Regular bed-time		68		32
Pocket money		20		80
Holiday as a family		98		2
Best friends (Ethnic group)		78	Indian	14 English; 8 West Ind
Visit to cinema		98	Indian Films	2 English films
Type of music at home		60	Indian	2 English 38 mixed
Type of food at home		100	Indian	0 English

The responses regarding the provision of educational experiences are to be found in Table 5.12. Almost none of the boys have been to concerts or theatres, only a few possess materials which can help them to develop perceptual and spatial abilities. Only 24 per cent of the boys receive any help and encouragement in their school work. Twenty-two per cent of the families do not have any books at home, and the same percentage of boys do not have any books for their own use. Sixty-eight per cent of the boys have less than ten books and only four per cent of them spend money on books. Similar responses to other items lead us to infer that these boys do not get sufficient stimulation, encouragement and support from their parents which has been shown to be conducive to intellectual development (Vernon, 1969). From our personal impression, we gathered that these boys were bilingual; they could always be heard speaking in Punjabi/English in the school playgrounds. Our overall impression was that these boys were experiencing two cultures; the Punjabi culture at home and the English culture in school. These findings confirm the survey results reported in Chapter 4 on child-rearing practices.

Table 5.11: Percentage responses of British Punjabi boys indicating adherence to Punjabi culture

	Yes	*No*
Attendance at Gurdawara (Sikh temple)	96	4
Celebration of Indian festivals	90	10
Attendance at Sunday Punjabi school	38	62

Table 5.12: Percentage responses of British Punjabi boys on items relating to educational experiences

	Yes	*No*
Parents help and encouragement in school work	24	76
Library membership	80	20
Visits to theatres, concerts, etc.	2	98
Jigsaws at home	14	86
Tool-kit, model railways and blocks etc.	4	96
Games — Chess, Monopoly etc.	—	100
Spend pocket money on books	4	96
Choice of clothes	50	50
Visits to relatives or cinema on their own	14	86

	None	*(1-9)*	*(10-19)*	*(20-25)*	*(26 or more)*
Books at home	22	16	20	18	24
Books belonging to children (for their use)	22	68	6	—	4

To summarize, the families of our British Punjabi boys are still entrenched in their own culture and religion and have not adopted to any major extent the norms, values and language of the host community. Needless to say, understanding of the English ways of life, and to a degree, adoption of middle class life-style might be considered to be essential to secure the best education for their children. As has been shown in the discussion, the performance of these boys can in no way be substantially attributed to the cultural change in family life style, which remains essentially similar to the traditional Punjabi way of life. Therefore, I feel it is valid to ascribe their cognitive development to the nature and type of education which they have received in schools.

Our findings, in this respect, are in agreement with Prince (1968), Beard (1968), Pool (1968) and Lloyd (1971) who have also shown the importance of a Western-type education to the intellectual development of the children.

Summary of discussion

1. The thinking processes of the British Punjabi boys are very similar, both quantitatively and qualitatively, to that of the English boys, and this performance of the immigrant group is primarily due to the educational experiences they have had in English schools.

2. The senior boys of both the English and the British Punjabi samples do not perform significantly better than the junior boys of their respective cultural groups. This is explained as being due to the low-expectation syndrome.

3. The thinking processes of the indigenous Punjabi boys are markedly different, both qualitatively and quantitatively, from the British Punjabi boys; this is largely due to their poor educational experiences and to the rural environment in which they are being brought up.

4. The difference in performance between the two Punjabi groups (Indigenous/Immigrant) is more marked on the formally structured tests. This is due to lack of previous experience with the content and methodologies of the tests and lack of experience in doing tests.

5. The performance of the Punjabi sample is comparable to that of the British sample on the Conservation of Weight test; this anomalous result is attributed to their previous experience in measuring and weighing farm produce at home.

6. The results of this research indicate that the difference in performance of these two Punjabi groups (BP and P) arises primarily from the cultural and educational environments rather than genetic factors, as these were carefully controlled in this study. This supports the stance of Vernon (1967) and Cole *et al.* (1971) that prior to invoking genetic factors to explain intellectual development, we should examine closely the effect of socio-cultural milieux on cognitive processes.

Survey of Boys'and Girls' Opinions towards Acculturation

As we saw in the last chapter, the Punjabi family at home is largely unchanged in its customs and outlook. We have also seen that schooling in this country is having a marked effect on Punjabi children's perception and thinking styles. What I further wished to investigate was whether English schooling is having an effect on the way in which they regard their own culture and its relationship with that of the English. Since almost their only contact of any continuing length with the host culture is through school, any changes in the children's attitudes can probably be attributed to the influence of school.

For this investigation it was decided to work with secondary school students since they are both more conscious of their attitudes and are more able to articulate them; also, a questionnaire approach is possible when dealing with a large number. Very little research work has been done in this area except that of Evans (1971) and of Lewis (1970); other reports of attitudes and so on have been largely impressionistic accounts by teachers and community workers. As these young people's opinions on their own and English culture are very important, it was thought that this extra section is essential towards the fuller understanding of the Punjabi child.

Construction of the scale

It was decided to use a Likert-type scale, in which the subject is asked to express his degree of agreement or otherwise, on a five point scale, with a number of statements. A number of items relating to these adolescents' own culture and to English culture were assembled in the following categories:

1. Those relating to food and clothes.
2. Those relating to the rôle of women.

3. Those concerned with values and beliefs.
4. Those concerned with leisure and entertainment.
5. Those relating to community life.

Initially, 94 such items were presented to 16 judges for their comments on whether the items genuinely reflected the basic aspects of both cultures. Then 40 items which polarized were chosen, 20 from the 'Punjabi' end of the continuum and 20 from the 'English' end. Statements which most of the judges rated neutral or common to both cultures were rejected. For a preliminary small pilot study these 40 items were given to ten 15- and 16-year-olds, mainly to determine the linguistic suitablity of the items. Another six items were then rejected and the remaining scale of 34 items was given to 86 boys and girls, aged 14 to 16, in two Birmingham schools in a further pilot study. Item analysis was carried out by the standard procedures (Likert, 1932) and it was finally decided to keep 30 items, some of which were linguistically modified in view of the comments of the teachers and pupils Furthermore, factor analysis was done on the scale, though the details are too lengthy to be included here. However, any reader who is interested in the more technical details can contact me, and a research report is being prepared for publication. Of the 30 items, 14 sampled opinions on their own culture and 16 probed their attitude to English customs. Here are some examples:

Food   : Sometimes we should cook English food in our homes.
                          'I would rather eat our own food all the time'.
Role of women   : A woman's place is in the home.
                          'I wouldn't like to see our women behave like English women'.
Leisure   : Our films are more entertaining than English films.
                          'We (boys and girls) should be allowed to meet each other in Youth Clubs'.
Values and beliefs   : We should always try to fulfil our parents' wishes.
                          'Parents and children should live on their own and not with grandparents or uncles'.
                          Marriages should be arranged by the family.

(Some items are deliberately phrased negatively to avoid the development of a response-set).

(The full scale is to be found in Appendix B)

The sample

The Asian sample was taken from four Birmingham comprehensive schools whose immigrant population was more than 60 per cent. The 144 adolescents from the fourth, fifth and sixth Forms, were aged between 14 and 17 years and included some Gujuratis, Pakistani-Punjabis and Bengalis, but only the answers of the 98 Indian Punjabis were selected for detailed analysis. I am fully aware that it is generally accepted now that tests of attitude should be given by a person of the same ethnic group to elicit valid responses. However, it was decided that, as I was not personally known to the sample, the class teachers' closer acquaintance with the children might result in more truthful answers being given; the questionnaires were therefore given in all cases by the class teacher.

Analysis of the responses

The usual practice is to quantify the answers by giving a score of five to the 'strongly agree' category, three to 'undecided', one to 'strongly disagree', and four and two to the categories in-between. The numerical scores are then added to give a composite score to the scale or subscale as the case may be. However, this approach was rejected in favour of a qualitative approach for the following reasons: the numerical score blurs the differences in intensity because it gives an average score, and secondly, the special problem related to the 'undecided' category to whom a score of three is given. It is very difficult to say whether they are in the middle of the bi-polar continuum or whether they really don't know. On our scale there are quite a high proportion of such responses, particularly on some items, because of the nature of the likely conflict on some issues, e.g. 'Our customs and traditions are best for us'.

Discussion

The full details are set out in Table A.6 in Appendix A. Some items showed marked differences between boys' and girls' responses; they are discussed separately even though they may also belong to one of the following two categories which we shall discuss first:

A. Those which show acculturation to the host country.
B. Those which indicate adherence to their own culture.

The following table shows the 13 items in Category A in descending order of strength of feeling (Statements abbreviated).

Table 6.1: Acculturation items

Item No.		% Agreeing	% Don't Know	% Disagree
12	Should be allowed to choose own clothes	92	3	5
1	Girls and boys should be treated the same	91	5	4
15	Should cook English food	88	6	6
28	Should visit English cinemas, theatres	80	15	5
19	Should visit English homes	78	19	3
30	Like to make friends only with Punjabis	8	14	78
27	Only own doctors can understand us	18.3	13.3	68.4
8	Prefer to eat own food all the time	18.3	15.4	66.3
23	Feel very uneasy with the English	14.3	21.4	64.3
2	Should celebrate Christmas	62.2	14.3	23.5
18	Boys and girls should meet in clubs	57.2	20.4	12.3
9	Better to live with people from India	17.3	22.4	60.3
20	Prefer to live in area where other Indians are	20.4	22.4	57.2

This large number of items indicating a desire to acculturate (there are a further two — items 22 and 4 — from Table 6.3 which fall into this category as well), should be very encouraging to teachers in immigrant schools, since most of the items are concerned in one way or another with the school situation, which seems to have given the children a positive attitude to many aspects of English life. They are items which allow for a good deal of social acculturation but do not destroy their own culture: both can co-exist, e.g. the feeling that it is desirable to cook English food sometimes and rejection of the view that they should eat Indian food all the time indicates this quite clearly. Other items which indicate their approval of customs and social practices which they experience in school, e.g. the celebration of Christmas, independence training and the encouragement of individuality are reflected in their desire to meet each other in youth clubs and their very strong wish to be allowed to choose their own clothes. Although on the whole their answers show that, on balance, they do still regard their basic customs and traditions as best, they clearly do not wish to remain in ghetto-type areas (items 20,9) mixing only with others of their own group (items 30), but would like to be on social terms with the English community (items 28, 19, 23).

In this category no differentiation is made between the scores of boys and girls, although in all cases the degree of acculturation is greater for girls than for boys. The overall results, however, show favourable responses to acculturation. For the same reason, in the next table showing adherence to Punjabi culture, no difference is indicated, though in all items the boys showed a much stronger adherence to tradition than did the girls.

Table 6.2: Adherence to tradition items

Item No.		% Agree	% Undecided	% Disagree
14	Should learn to speak and write Punjabi	89	6	5
25	Should ignore our own language to get on here	6	6	88
3	Do not wish to go back to India	16	9	75
16	Should alter names so that teachers can say them	12	14	74
6	Should always try to fulfill parents wishes	68.3	18.4	13.3
24	Should be more inter-marriages	21	24	55
21	Our films are the more entertaining	53	22.5	24.5

It would seem from this table that both boys and girls do wish to retain their cultural identity by retaining those facets which are at the core of that identity, namely their language, their names, which are chosen from the religious texts and which are very different from English names, and by keeping strong links with their own country of origin or ancestry. Though they wish to mix socially with young English people of both sexes, they do not wish to be assimilated into the host culture through inter-marriage. Items 5 and 13 (Table 63) also come into this category showing adherence, but due to the significant difference between boys' and girls' responses they are tabled below. It may be noted that there is a large number of 'undecided' responses in these items relating to traditions reflecting the inevitable ambivalence with which these youngsters, who are at present living in two separate milieux, are coming to regard their own culture.

In the following table the percentages of various responses are not given, so that it may be clearly shown where the boys' and girls' answers are radically different. On all these items boys were significantly different from girls; the chi-square test was used to establish these differences.

These differences, in my view, are due to the different rôle-expectations of boys and girls in the Punjabi community. Whereas boys retain their male advantages (not a uniquely Punjabi affair!) through the retention of traditional ways, girls feel that there is a lot to be

Table 6.3: Different opinions between boys and girls

Item No.		Girls	Boys
29	Men should make all the family decisions	Reject	Accept
22	Marriages should be arranged by family	Reject	Balanced
17	It is good to learn about Christianity	Accept	Balanced
13	Our women should wear English clothes	Balanced	Reject
11	A woman's place is in the home	Totally Reject	Accept
10	People should not live in an extended family	Accept	Reject
5	Our own customs and traditions are best	Balanced	Accept
4	Our boys and girls should go out with the English	Balanced	Accept

gained in terms of individual freedom by adopting the English concept of relative equality of the sexes. It may be remembered that in the two previous tables the girls were more for acculturation and less in favour of tradition; the boys showed much more adherence to tradition and less desire to acculturate, especially on those items relating to women's rôle. Complete polarization occurred on items 11: 'A woman's place is in the home', and 29: 'Men should make all family decisions'. Item 4 is the odd-man-out on the scale, because it is the only item on which boys show the greater degree of acculturation and, without further information, it is very difficult to explain. Items 7 and 26 have not been categorized as the responses showed that they were not useful items: 26 because of ambiguity and 7 because the popularity of school dinners is doubtful, for whatever reasons, even amongst English children.

The overall results are in line with the only research which is known to me, that of Evans (1971) which is an analysis of a Marplan survey in Southall in 1971. He found that Indian youths, whilst retaining their own cultural identify, would like to be acquainted and live in harmony with English customs and society — 78 per cent feeling that they should make an effort to adapt to these customs.

In the main project of this book it was shown that the school had a very great influence on the ways in which children think and solve problems. In this investigation into attitudes it has again ben found that school has a significant influence, this time in building up a positive attitude to the host culture. What also emerges is that children wish to retain the essential elements of their own identity and the schools should now provide courses in their own language, history, geography and religion. It is strange to note that in only one of the four schools where this investigation was conducted was there a course offered in Punjabi; the others were giving French or German. When this was pointed out to the school it was said that courses in the children's own language would present too many problems because of the number of Indian languages. This aspect is much over-played in this country and provides a good excuse for not bothering. After all, there are remarkably few large groups of Indians speaking different languages in this country: most speak either Urdu or Punjabi and they are mostly concentrated in very large groups. There are also some Gujuratis and Bengalis but they are in sizeable clusters, too. Even if it is not possible for some reason to provide courses in the two major languages, an acceptable alternative for all groups would be Hindi, which is the national language of the Indian sub-continent and which is the second language of many millions, besides being the first language of a far larger number.

Names, too, are an important part of life and a child's name is as much a part of his self-image as his face. To some, it may seem to be an unimportant point, but from the opinion expressed through item 2 — on names — the Anglicization of Punjabi names is clearly unpopular, as is the rather widespread mispronounciation of these names which can lead to embarrassment and annoyance.

In this chapter, we have seen that it is clear that these young Indians very much want to spend some leisure time in youth clubs and perhaps the schools could try and involve them in such activities, bearing in mind that parents will have to be convinced that nothing occurs at youth clubs which could compromise their high ideals of deportment which they have, particularly concerning the girls. Perhaps it would be possible to explain to the parents in circulars written in the appropriate language, the aims, purposes and activities of youth clubs in an effort to overcome their natural anxieties.

I am absolutely certain from my own personal experience that Punjabis wish to preserve their religion from which they derive their moral and spiritual strength to cope with day-to-day problems of living in this country. At the present time most young Indians, unlike perhaps the adolescent English, are actively involved and interested in religion and it would be very useful for mutual respect if Sikhism, Islam and Hinduism could be included as a normal part of the Religious Education syllabus. This might lead to some understanding of the eating and dressing customs of immigrant groups, which seem as yet to be as much of a mystery to most city dwellers as they were when the immigrants arrived.

To contribute towards racial harmony, a truly multi-cultural approach is urgently required in urban schools, which presents the culture of the immigrant groups as a viable and respectable way of life. To do this we need to use the resources both of the children and of the thousands of teachers from all the immigrant groups, whose special possible contribution to this field is all-too-often left untapped.

Conclusions

The purpose of this monograph was to study the social-cultural background of the Punjabi Sikh children, who now form a large part of many city communities, in relation to their intellectual development.

That the Punjabi attitudes to child-rearing haven't substantially changed is apparent from the research reported in Chapter 3: changes which have taken place have been in their attitude to the physical and emotional comfort of the young babies, i.e. regarding feeding and sleeping. In the areas which affect educational attainment little or nothing has altered.

The Punjabis who have had full schooling in this country showed a similar pattern of abilities to that of their English schoolmates; their performance, as we have discussed in Chapter, 5, is primarily due to their school-based educational experiences. Thus the result of the study is encouraging to those educationists who stress the important role of school in the intellectual development of the children.

One of the findings of the study was that for these children the only contact with the host culture was in schools. This is probably the only institution where they interact face-to-face with English children and adults, and where they have access to the intellectual, affective, social and moral codes of the English culture; it is the sole agency for socializing the children into the host culture: and from Chapter 6 it is clear that schools are indeed changing young people's attitudes and fostering a positive attitude to English culture. So it follows that a resonable balance between the numbers of native and immigrant pupils in schools should be maintained, to provide enough opportunity for effective interaction; schools with a very high proportion of immigrant children might lose the kind of ethos which in our view is necessary to some understanding and acquisition of the English way of life. In the schools from which our samples were tested, the number of immigrant children (at least 60 per cent) was far higher than I personally consider desirable. Needless to say, the teaching staff employed in these schols should have a sympathetic attitude towards and some appreciation of the cultural background of these children, which, as we have explained in Chapter 3, is different from their own. This would, in my view, lead to better mutual understanding between school and home.

A healthy partnership between school and parents is now widely regarded as essential to develop the full potential of the children. From my own personal knowledge of the Punjabi family and the data relating to the home background of these children, it can confidently be said that parents do not, or cannot, participate in the life of the school (see also Townsend, 1972). This we feel is the result of their inability to communicate in English and their fear of authority. Furthermore, I think that though the Punjabi family values education highly, it does not fully appreciate the rôle which parents have to play in the fuller development and educational progress of the children. As one parent remarked to me during a visit to a family: 'Education takes place in school and not at home' (sic). Thus, I feel that the head teacher and staff of these schools have the additional task of gaining the confidence and co-operation of the parents. The appointment of educational social workers with relevant ethnic backgrounds is particularly important and would facilitate the development of such confidence and co-operation.

The data from the child-rearing study and the interview with the Punjabi boys clearly demonstrated the lack of perceptual, linguistic and educational experiences of the children provided by the family. Therefore, it is important for the schools with a high intake of immigrant pupils to provide such experiences before proceeding to teach the more formal aspects of the school curriculum — even when the immigrant children are far beyond infant school age.

There has been no research, known to me, designed to assess the attitude of immigrant parents to education. Such a study would be illuminating and specific questions for this type of inquiry might be formulated along the following lines:

1. How far are immigrant parents aware of the structure and function of the English system of education?
2. What is their concept of education — especially with regard to the non-academic part of the curriculum, bearing in mind their own experience of a very formal, academic type of schooling?
3. What is their attitude to the adoption of any English norms and conventions?

One of the most surprising findings of our study was that the older British boys, of both ethnic groups, did not perform significantly better than the younger boys: this has been explained as a result of the low-expectation syndrome. The implications of these results are serious enough to merit a further study with a large sample from Educational Priority Area schools to provide further support or otherwise for this finding.

To conclude this section we now briefly consider the implication for the teaching of the English language. If we accept the important role of language in the development of higher cognitive processes, further attention has to be paid to the improvement of the children's oral and written language. (A recent report by McEwen *et al.* (1975) has shown clearly the poor performance of immigrant children in listening, reading and writing). Special classes in those schools where the proportion of immigrant children exceeds (say 20 per cent) of the total population, are vitally important to as full as possible an understanding of the English language, because such classes do not presuppose a background of comprehension in English. The common practice of removing children from an ordinary class for instruction by a peripatetic teacher is unsatisfactory, as no continuity is maintained on return to the normal class. From my own experience I found that special classes were more beneficial, not only from the point of view of learning but also are more rewarding to the teacher. The research work (James, 1972) of the Faculty of Education at Aberystwyth with Welsh-speaking play groups and nursery classes has clearly shown the benefits which accrue from the teaching of a second language at a very early age — from three years onwards. The children, even from wholly English backgrounds, rapidly acquired competence in comprehension and spoken Welsh. We feel that this experience demonstrates the value of an English-speaking situation for immigrant children for some part of the day, in the pre-school years: provision of playgroups in immigrant enclaves, such as Handsworth in Birmingham, would pay dividends both in the short-term goal of fluent spoken English and later in improved scholastic achievement, by bringing children into close contact with the English language at the age when they are most receptive to new linguistic experiences.

Arising from our research, we suggest the further following ideas for investigation:

1. As far as home background is concerned, our semi-structured interview should be refined into a questionnaire and statistically validated for future use.
2. Attempts should be made to investigate the divergent thinking abilities of this cultural group, as no such test was included in our battery.
3. It may also be interesting to sample the range of abilities of the immigrant children by using group tests and basing the study on the psychometricians' concept of mental abilities.

4. In recent years, bilingualism and its relationship to intellectual development has attracted a great deal of attention. Asian children are in an interesting position: they acquire their native language at home, but do not usually receive any formal instruction in it. It would be illuminating to study the effect of oral linguisticability on their performance with cognitive problems. Furthermore, it should be interesting to study the effect of the native language on subsequent learning of English. An extensive project on these lines is being undertaken with Welsh children at the University College of Wales, Aberystwyth.

5. Our research has shown that boys are adopting modes of thinking which are more akin to the European culture than their family background. Research is needed to identify the problems of adjustment, especially during adolescence, that these children may be experiencing.

Finally, let us consider the implications of our research findings for the education of the indigenous Punjabi children. Observations were made both on the actual thinking processes and general attitude to thinking of the samples. As reported earlier the boys in our samples were perceptually orientated, rigid in their thinking and tended to use the ostensive mode to communicate their ideas. Their general attitude to thinking is summed up in the following remark made by one of the older boys: 'Please, we do not think — but do as our teacher tells us to do' (sic). The validity of this type of attitude was confirmed by the long pauses, dumb silences and perplexed looks, when asked the question: 'What do you think?'

Our study of the British Punjabi boys convinced us about the important value of the educational experiences provided by the English school. Hence it is not unreasonable to direct our attention to the quality of education which the indigenous Punjabi boys receive in their primary schools. As discussed earlier (Chapter 3) the primary schools in Punjab are run on mechanistic lines and consequently provide no scope for children to enhance their understanding and develop their thinking abilities. I feel that the curriculum, teaching methods, and the attitude of the teachers to children in these schools deserve serious appraisal if education is to promote understanding and critical thinking.

But before we discuss these aspects of school, the sceptics have to be answered who argue that schools only mirror the values, beliefs and indeed the type of 'rationalities' practised by the population outside the school. Hence they believe it is not legitimate to expect these institutions to provide experiences which are not in sympathy and/or at variance with the cultural pattern of the community.

We feel that this view is too conservative a view of education especially in democratically run countries. In such countries education and other institutions have to play their part in bringing about changes in people's attitudes, beliefs and values, as innovation by social and/or political revolution is not considered legitimate.

The curriculum of Punjabi primary schools is too narrow; excessive emphasis is placed on teaching the 3Rs. Subjects such as craft, art, physical education, local history and geography are not included in the school activities. The indigenous forms of thought, and modes of experiences which are enshrined in folk-poetry, drama, myth, religious texts and folk tales are rarely taught. The teachers are solely concerned in teaching, through the most formal method, the basic rudiments of subjects, and ignore the rich reservoir of Punjabi culture. We are quite aware of the criticism that formal type of reasonings — 'rationalities' — may be at variance with the children's experience and may cause psychological conflict and anxiety. But, if the attitude orientation of the teachers is sympathetic, then such difficulties can be overcome.

The major changes, however, have to be undertaken in the field of teaching methods. Children are taught by drill method and consequently learn everything by rote. No direct perceptual and conceptual experiences are provided to develop their understanding. Needless to say, children at the primary school stage (concrete thinking stage) mainly learn through first-hand experiences; they need to discover rules and principles for themselves and engage in practical activities when learning science, geography and other subjects. The importance of immediate practical experience such as touching, seeing and manipulation of material cannot be over-emphasized.

The attitudes of teachers towards the children will have to be radically re-orientated if we expect the future Punjabi children to be intellectually curious and questioning. Teachers have to stop treating children as 'little slaves', who are there to carry out their commands and wishes instantaneously. They have to learn to respect the children and also have a patient and sympathetic attitude to their perceptions and judgements. Indeed, an authoritarian attitude has to be replaced by a democratic one.

The reform of these three areas can only come about if the training of teachers is radically restructured. They themselves suffer from some of the disadvantages mentioned earlier, e.g. rote learning of prescribed text books. We feel that the exchange of university and training colleges staff with western countries would be a step in this direction. At present Commonwealth bursaries for serving teachers in under-developed countries are the main channel through which experienced teachers have the chance to broaden their knowledge.

Arising from our research, here are some specific questions which can be further investigated:

1. Replication of our work with girls, by a female research worker, to assess the differences in performance between the boys and girls, and to see if the same relationships exist within the girls' samples as were found operative within the boys'.

2. We feel that there is a need to assess the abilities of these children by using an extended battery of Piagetian tests which can be easily adapted.

3. Comparison of illiterate non-school-going children with school-going children to assess the importance of school in intellectual development.

4. An experimental study to assess the efficiency of modern methods of teaching (discovery method, etc.) with the Punjabi children.

5. Research is needed to construct objective tests of intelligence and 'aptitudes', with indigenous material, for diagnostic and prognostic purposes.

ASHBY, B., MORRISON, A. and BUTCHER, H.J. (1970) 'The Abilities and Attainments of Immigrant Children,' *Research in Education*, 4 (Nov.) 73—80.

BATH, S.K. (1970) 'Educational Progress of the Punjabi Immigrant Pupils' Unpublished MEd thesis, U.C. Wales, Aberystwyth.

BEARD, R.M. (1968) 'An Investigation into Mathematical Concepts among Ghanaian Children,' *Teacher Education*, May 1968, 9—14 and Nov. 1968, 132—45.

BEARD, R.M. (1972) *An Outline of Piaget's Developmental Psychology*. London: Routledge and Kegan Paul.

BERNSTEIN, B. (1971) *Class, Codes and Control*. Vol. I. London: Routledge and Kegan Paul.

BERRY, J.W. (1965) 'Temne and Eskimo Perceptual Skills,' *Int. J. Psychol.*, 1, 27—229.

BING, E. (1965) 'Effects of Child Rearing Practices on Development of Differential Cognitive Styles,' *Child Development*, 34, 631—648.

BRUNER, J.S., OLVER, R.R. and GREENFIELD, M.P. (1967a) *Studies in Cognitive Growth*. London: Wiley.

BRUNER, J.S., GOODNOW, J.J. and AUSTIN, A.G. (1967b) *A Study of Thinking*. New York, Science Edition, Inc.

BRUNER, J.S. (1967c) 'On the Conservation of Liquids.' In Bruner, J.S. *et al. Studies in Cognitive Growth*. London: John Wiley and Sons.

BULLOCK, A. (Sir) (1975) *A Language for Life*. London: HMSO.

BURROUGHS, G.E.R. (1971) 'Design and Analysis in Educational Research.' Educn. Monograph No. 8. Birmingham, Univ. School of Education.

BUTCHER, H.J. (1972) 'Comments on Jensen's Paper,' *Educ. Research*, 14, 2, 94.

CHIU, LIAN-HWANG (1972) 'A cross-cultural comparison of cognitive styles in Chinese and American Children' *Int. J. Psychol.*, 7, 235—243.

COLE, M., GAY, J., GLICK, A.J. and SHARP, W.D. (1971) *The Cultural Context of Learning and Thinking*. London: Methuen.

CROFT, M. (Ed.) (1970) *Family, Class and Education*: a reader. London: Longman.

DASEN, P.P. (1972) *'The Development of Conservation in Aboriginal Children'* A Replication Study, *Int. J. Psychol.*, 7, 2, 75—85.

DAVEY, A.G. (1968) 'The Tristan da Cunha Children's Concept of Equivalence,' *Brit. J. Educ. Psychol.*, 38, 2, p. 163—70.

DAWSON, J.L.M. (1967) 'Cultural and Physiological influences on Spatial-perceptual Processes in West-Africa,' I—II, *Int. J. Psychol.*, 115—28; 171—85.

DE LEMOS, M.M. (1969) 'The Development of Conservation in Aboriginal Children,' *Int. J. Psychol.*, 4, 255—269.

DOUGLAS, J.W.B. (1964) *The Home and the School.* London: MacGibbon and Kee.

DOSANJH, J. (1969) 'Punjabi Immigrant Children: their Social and Educational problems.' Educ. papers no. 10, Nottingham University School of Education.

ELKIND, D. (1968) 'Conservation and Concept formation.' In Elkind, D. and Flavell, J.H. *Studies in Cognitive Development* p. 171—90. London: OUP.

EVANS, L.J. and SEGALL, H.M. (1969) 'Learning to Classify by Colour and by Function: A Study of Concept Discovery by Ganda Children,' *J. of Soc. Psychol.*, 77, Feb. 1969, 35—53.

EVANS, P., (1971) *Attitudes of Young Immigrants.* London: Runnymede Trust.

EYSENCK H.J. (1971) *Race, Intelligence and Education.* London: Temple-Smith.

FOGELMAN, K.R. (1971) *Piagetian Tests for the Primary School.* London: NFER.

GHUMAN, A.S. (1974) 'A cross-cultural study of the Basic Thinking Processes of English, "British" Punjabi and Indigenous Punjabi Boys'. PhD. thesis, University of Birmingham.

GOODNOW, J.J. (1962) 'A Test of Milieu Effects with some of Piaget's Tasks,' *Psych. Mongr.*, 76. No 239.

GOODNOW, J.J. (1969) 'Cultural variations in Cognitive Skills.' In Williams, R.D. *Cross-cultural Studies.* Harmondsworth: Penguin Books.

GOUGH, H.G. (1949) 'A Short Social Status Inventory,' *J. Ed. Psychol.*, 40, 52—6.

GREEN, R.D., FORD, P.M. and FLAMER, B.G. (Eds. 1971). *Measurement and Piaget.* London: McGraw Hill.

GREENFIELD, M.P. and BRUNER, J.S. (1966) 'Culture and Cognitive Growth,' *Int. J. Psychol.*, 1, 2, 89—107.

GRIFFITH, A. (1971) 'Some recent Researches on the Social Determinants of Education.' An Annotated Bibliography. Leeds: University of Leeds, Institute of Education.

HARRIS, B.D. (1963) *Goodenough-Harris Drawing Test Manual.* London: Harcourt, Bruce and World.

HAYNES, J.M. (1971) *Educational Assessment of Immigrant Pupils.* London: NFER.

HYDE, D.M. (1959) 'An Investigation of Piaget's Theories of the Development of the Concept of Number.' Unpub. PhD thesis, University of London.

INHELDER, B. (1971) 'Developmental theory and Diagnostic Procedures.' In Green, R.D. *et al. Measurement and Piaget.*

JAMES, D.L. (1972) 'The Second Penparcau School Project in Early Bilingualism.' Bulletin No. 19, Collegiate Faculty of Education. U.C. Wales Aberystwyth.

JENSEN, A. (1971) 'Do Schools Cheat Minority Children?' *Educ. Res.*, 14, 1, 3—28.

JENSEN, A. (1972) *Genetics and Education.* London: Methuen.

LESSER, G.S., FIFER, G. and CLARK, D.H. (1965) 'Mental Abilities of Children from different Social-class and Cultural Groups.' Monog. Society for Research in Child Development, No. 30, 1965.

LEWIS, E.G. (1970) 'Immigrants, their language and Development,' *Trends in Education,* 19.

LIKERT, R. (1932) 'A Technique for the Measurement of Attitudes,' *Archives Psychology,* No. 140.

LITTLE, A., MABEY, C. and WHITKER, G. (1968) 'The Education of Immigrant Pupils in Inner London Primary Schools,' *Race,* 9,4.

LLOYD, B.B. (1971) 'Studies of Conservation with Yoruba Children of Differing Ages and Experience.' *Child Development,* 42, 1, 416—28.

LLOYD, F. and PIDGEON, D.A. (1961) 'An Investigation into the Effects of Coaching on Non-verbal Test Material with European, Indian and African Children,' *Brit. J. Educ. Psychol.*, 31, 145—51.

LOVELL, K. (1961) *The Growth of Mathematical and Scientific Concepts in Children.* Uni Books: University of London Press.

LUNN, J.C.B. (1970) *Streaming in the Primary School.* London: NFER.

LUNZER, E.A. (1973) *Recent Studies in Britain based on the work of Jean Piaget.* Slough: NFER.

MACFARLANE SMITH, I. (1964) *Spatial Ability.* London: University London Press.

MACCOBY, M. and MODIANO, N. (1967) 'On Culture and Equivalence: In Bruner, J.S. *et al. Studies in Cognitive Growth.* New York: John Wiley.

MACCOBY, M. and MODIANO, N. (1969) 'Cognitive Styles in Rural and Urban Mexico,' *Human Development,* 12, 1, 22—33.

MCEWEN, E. *et al.* (1975) *Language Proficiency in the Multi-Racial Junior School,* Slough: NFER.

MCFIE, J. and THOMPSON, J.A. (1970) 'Intellectual Abilities of Immigrant Children.' 40, 3, p. 348—51.

MCFIE, J. (1961) 'The Effect of Education on African Performance in a group of Intellectual tests,' *Brit. J. Educ. Psychol.*, 31, 232—40.

NEHRU, J. (1946) *The Discovery of India.* London: Meridian Books Ltd.

OLVER, R.R. and HORNSBY, R.J. (1967) 'On Equivalence.' In: Bruner, J. *et al. Studies in Cognitive Growth.* London: John Wiley & Sons.

PEEL, E.A. (1960) *The Pupil's Thinking* (p. 43). London: Oldbourne.

PELUFFO, N. (1967) 'Culture and Cognitive Problems,' *Int. J. Psych.*, 2, 187—198.

PHILP, H. and KELLY, M. (1947) 'Product and Process in Cognitive Development: Some Comparative Data on the Performance of School Age Children in Different Cultures,' *Brit. J. Educ. Psych.*, 44, 3, p. 248—265.

PIAGET, J. (1952) *The Child's Concept of Number.* London: Routledge and Kegan Paul.

PIAGET, J. (1956) *Logic and Psychology.* Manchester: Manchester University Press.

PIAGET, J. (1966) 'Necessité et Signification des Recherches Génétiques,' *Int. J. Psych.*, 1, 1, 3—13.

PIDGEON, D.A. (1970) *Expectation and Pupil Performance.* Slough: NFER.

POOL, H.E. (1968) 'The Effect of Urbanisation upon Scientific Concept attainment among Haussa Children of Northern Nigeria,' *Brit. J. Educ. Psychol.*, 38, 1, 57—63.

PRICE-WILLIAMS, D., GORDON, W. and RAMIREZ, M. (1967) 'Skill and Conservation: A Study of Pottery-making Children.' Special Report (III) Rice University, USA.

PRINCE, J.R. (1968) 'The Effect of Western Education on Science Conceptualization in New Guinea,' *Brit. J. Educ. Psychol.*, 38, 64—74.

RAVEN, J.C. (1965) 'Guide to using Coloured Progressive Matrices.' London: H.K. Lewis and Co.

RICHARDSON, K. and SPEARS, D. (Edt. 1972) *Race, Culture and Intelligence.* London: Penguin Books Ltd.

SAINT, C.K. (1963) 'Scholastic and Sociological Adjustment Problems of the Punjabi Speaking Children in Smethwick.' Unpub. MEd. thesis. University of Birmingham.

SEMENOFF, B. and LAIRD, A.J. (1952) 'The Vygotsky Test as a Measure of Intelligence,' *Brit. J. Psychol.*, 43, 94—102.

SEMENOFF, B. and TRIST, E. (1958) *Diagnostic Performance Tests.* London: Tavistock, p. 15—16.

SERPELO, R. (1969) 'Cultural Differences in Attentional Preferences for Colour over Form,' *Int. J. Psychol.*, 4, 1, 1—8.

SHARMA, R. (1971) 'The Measured Intelligence of Children from the Indian Sub-Continent.' Unpub. PhD thesis, University of London.

SHARMA, U. (1971) *Rampal and his Family.* London: Collins.

STONES, E. and HESLOP, R.J. (1968). 'The Formation and Extension of Class Concepts in Primary School Children,' *Brit. J. Educ. Psychol.*, 38, Nov. 1968, 261—71.

STOTT, D.H. (1960) 'Interaction of Heredity and Environment in regard to Measured Intelligence.' In: Butcher, J.H. and Lomax, E.B. Eds. *Readings in Human Intelligence.* London: Methuen.

TOWNSEND, H.E.R. and BRITTON, M.E. (1972) *Organization in Multi-racial Schools* Slough: NFER.

VERNON, P.E. (1965) 'Environmental handicaps and Intellectual Development,' *Brit. J. Educ. Psychol.*, 35, 9—20; 117—26.

VERNON, P.E. (1969) *Intelligence and Cultural Environment.* London: Methuen.

VYGOTSKY, S.L. (1962) *Thought and Language.* Massachusetts: MIT.

WECHSLER, D. (1949) *WISC Manual: Intelligence Scale for Children.* New York: The Psychological Corporation.

WHORF, B.L. (1956) *Language, Thought and Reality.* Cambridge, Massachusetts: M.I.T. Press.

WITKIN, H.A., DYK, R.B., FATERSON, H.F., GOODENOUGH, D.R. and KARP, S.A. (1962). *Psychological Differentiation.* New York: Wiley.

WITKIN, H.A. (1966) 'Cognitive Styles and Cross-Cultural Research,' *Int. J. Psychol.*, 2, 233—49.

WITKIN, H.A. *et al.* (1974) 'Social Conformity and Psychological Differentiation,' *Int. J. Psychol.*, 9, I, p. 11—31.

Appendix A

Table A.1: Ages of boys. Mean age and 'range' of the samples

		Mean Age	Range	No.
1.	English junior	10 years 4.3 months	12 months	25
2.	English senior	11 years 3.2 months	10 months	25
3.	British Punjabi junior	10 years 3.5 months	13 months	25
4.	British Punjabi senior	11 years 5 months	10 months	25
5.	Punjabi junior	10 years 3 months	12 months	20
6.	Punjabi senior	11 years 6.6 months	8 months	20

Table A.2: Social class categories of the English and the British Punjabi samples

		6	5	4	3	
English	(9 - 9+)	15	5	3	2	
	(11+)	15	4	4	2	
		30	9	7	4	= 50
British Punjabi	9 (9 - 9+)	19	3	1	2	
	(11+)	18	5	1	1	
		37	8	2	2	= 50

The categories in the classification refer to the following occupations (12).

Class 6   unskilled manual workers
Class 5   personal service and semi-skilled manual workers
Class 4   clerical workers, shop assistants and skilled manual workers
Class 3   shopkeepers and foremen

Table A.3: Multivariate analyses of variance on six groups

Groups	No. of Variables	DF	Wilks' Lambda	F	P
a) EJ v ES v BPJ v BPS v PJ v PS	5	F1 = 25.00 F2 = 484.43	0.328	6.78	<0.001
b) EJ v ES v BPJ v BPS	5	F1 = 15 F2 = 254.37	0.816	1.30	N.S.
c) EJ+S v BPJ+S v PJ+S	5	F1 = 10.0 F2 = 266.00	0.389	16.06	<.001
d) EJ+S v BPJ+S	5	F1 = 5.00 F2 = 94.00	0.928	1.46	N.S.
e) EJ+S v PJ+S	5	F1 = 5.0 F2 = 84.00	0.284	42.30	<.001
f) BPJ+S v PJ+S	5	F1 = 5.00 F2 = 84.00	0.393	25.95	<.001
g) EJ v ES v BPJ v BPS	7	F1 = 21.50 F2 = 258.98	0.703	1.61	<.05
h) EJ+S v BPJ+S	7	F1 = 7.00 F2 = 92.00	0.829	2.71	<.05

Table A4: Means and standard deviations of bonus marks gained on WISC Block Design Test

	Mean	SD	SE	N
E_{J+S}	2.900	2.975	.420	50
BP_{J+S}	2.760	3.346	.474	50
P_{J+S}	None of the boys earned any bonus marks			

Note: CR = .22 Hence no significant difference exists between the British Punjabi (BP_{J+S}) and the English (E_{J+S}) boys.

Table A.5: Performance of British Punjabi and English samples on the Conservation Tests

Succession :	3	2	1	None	N
BP_J	6	7	5	7	25
BP_S	7	11	2	5	25
E_J	11	2	6	6	25
E_S	8	7	5	5	25

Table A.6: Responses of boys and girls to the survey of opinions

Item	1 B	1 G	2 B	2 G	3 B	3 G	4 B	4 G	5 B	5 G	6 B	6 G	7 B	7 G	8 B	8 G	9 B	9 G	10 B	10 G
Strongly Disagree	0	0	4	6	24	20	5	15	5	5	0	2	2	5	5	9	5	14	3	10
Disagree	4	0	4	9	13	16	2	11	3	14	2	9	23	19	19	32	19	21	16	0
Undecided	5	0	7	7	3	6	10	8	10	18	3	15	8	16	6	9	6	16	15	11
Agree	15	14	19	25	1	3	14	13	14	11	22	21	7	13	10	5	10	3	7	20
Strongly Agree	19	41	9	8	2	10	12	8	11	7	16	8	3	2	3	0	3	1	2	14

Table A.6: continued

Item	11 B	11 G	12 B	12 G	13 B	13 G	14 B	14 G	15 B	15 G	16 B	16 G	17 B	17 G	18 B	18 G	19 B	19 G	20 B	20 G
Strongly Disagree	1	28	2	1	8	2	2	0	2	0	28	23	8	2	1	1	2	0	5	14
Disagree	12	22	0	2	18	16	3	0	3	1	7	14	12	9	5	5	1	0	16	21
Undecided	7	2	0	3	12	19	4	2	4	2	3	11	3	18	10	10	9	10	10	12
Agree	14	2	17	17	2	10	15	23	28	39	2	4	17	19	15	14	24	26	8	4
Strongly Agree	9	1	24	32	3	8	19	30	6	13	3	3	3	7	12	25	7	19	4	4

Table A.6: Continued

Item	21 B	21 G	22 B	22 G	23 B	23 G	24 B	24 G	25 B	25 G	26 B	26 G	27 B	27 G	28 B	28 G	29 B	29 G	30 B	30 G
Strongly Disagree	1	9	9	21	10	16	24	13	30	22	11	6	13	20	3	1	3	34	15	28
Disagree	7	7	9	13	13	24	6	11	11	23	9	10	17	17	1	0	7	12	20	13
Undecided	13	9	6	11	12	9	4	19	0	6	5	21	3	10	7	8	10	4	6	8
Agree	10	9	9	5	8	5	4	7	2	3	7	17	7	3	21	30	12	1	2	3
Strongly Agree	12	21	10	5	0	1	5	5	0	1	11	1	3	5	11	16	11	4	0	3

Appendix B

B.1: List of items used in the Equivalence Test.

1. Bee; Double-garage; Buffalo; Screw; Raincoat; Pumpkin; Hammer.
2. Carrots; Lamp; Clock; Frog; House; Sword; Car.
3. Dogs; Parrot; Water-pump; Weighing Scales; Boots; Plant; Rabbit.
4. Umbrella; Saw; Shoe; Bicycle; Pair of Scissors; Sun; Radio.
5. Aeroplane; Tree; Doll; Coin; Train; Ruler; Apple.
6. Balloons; Comb; Gloves; Farmyard; Candle; Pancake; Nails.

B.2: List of items on which semi-structured interview was based.

Name: Class:

School: Date:

1. Father's occupation:
2. Mother at work:
3. Children in the family:
4. Nuclear or extended family:
5. Language spoken by parents:
6. Language with parents:
7. Language with siblings:
8. Newspaper, if any:
9. Attendance at Gurdawara (Sikh temple):
10. Attendance at Punjabi school:
11. Use of local library (membership):
12. Visits to theatre, concerts etc:
13. Regular bed-time:
14. Own room:
15. Birthday celebration:
16. Celebration of festivals:
    a) Christmas:
    b) Indian:
17. Pocket money:
18. Best friends:
19. Type of food at home:
20. Visit to cinema:
21. Type of music:
22. Visits to English homes:
23. Visits from English people:
24. Parents' help in home-work:
25. Jigsaws at home:
26. Tool-kit, model railways etc:
27. Games — Chess, Monopoly etc:
28. Books at home:
29. Books for their use:
30. Pocket money on books:
31. Choice of clothes:
32. Visit to relatives or cinema on their own:
33. Holiday as a family:

Table B.3

1. Girls and boys should be treated the same ....SA A U D SD
2. We should celebrate Christmas as we celebrate our own religious festivals ....SA A U D SD
3. I have no wish to go back to the country that my parents came from ....SA A U D SD
4. I would like to see boys and girls from our community going out with English boys and girls ....SA A U D SD
5. Our own customs and traditions are best for us ....SA A U D SD
6. We should always try to fulfil our parents' wishes ....SA A U D SD
7. We should stay for school dinners ....SA A U D SD
8. I would rather eat our own food all the time ....SA A U D SD
9. We are better off living with people from our own countries SA A U D SD
10. Parents and children should live on their own and not with grandparents and uncles ....SA A U D SD
11. A woman's place is in the home ....SA A U D SD
12. We should be allowed to choose our own clothes ....SA A U D SD
13. Our women should wear English clothes ....SA A U D SD
14. We should learn to speak and write our own language ....SA A U D SD
15. Sometimes we should cook English food in our homes ....SA A U D SD
16. We should alter our names so that our teachers can say them easily ....SA A U D SD
17. It is good for us to learn something about Christianity ....SA A U D SD
18. We (boys and girls) should be allowed to meet each other in youth clubs ....SA A U D SD
19. We should visit the homes of our English friends ....SA A U D SD
20. I would prefer to live in an area where there are families from our own community ....SA A U D SD
21. Our films are more entertaining than English films ....SA A U D SD
22. Marriages should be arranged by the family ....SA A U D SD
23. I feel very uneasy with the English ....SA A U D SD
24. There should be more marriages between our people and the English ....SA A U D SD
25. We should ignore our own language if we want to get on in this country ....SA A U D SD
26. I would not like our women to behave like English women .SA A U D SD
27. Only our own doctors can understand our illnesses ....SA A U D SD
28. We should visit English cinemas and play houses ....SA A U D SD
29. Men should make all the decisions about the affairs of the family ....SA A U D SD
30. I would only like to make friends with my own countrymen .SA A U D SD